1 MONTH OF
FREE
READING

at

www.ForgottenBooks.com

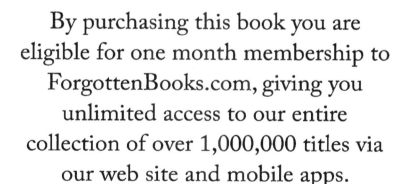

By purchasing this book you are eligible for one month membership to ForgottenBooks.com, giving you unlimited access to our entire collection of over 1,000,000 titles via our web site and mobile apps.

To claim your free month visit:

www.forgottenbooks.com/free790747

ISBN 978-0-483-59800-3
PIBN 10790747

For support please visit www.forgottenbooks.com

THE OUTLOOK
FOR AMERICAN PROSE

THE UNIVERSITY OF CHICAGO PRESS
CHICAGO, ILLINOIS

THE BAKER & TAYLOR COMPANY
NEW YORK

THE MACMILLAN COMPANY OF CANADA, LIMITED
TORONTO

THE CAMBRIDGE UNIVERSITY PRESS
LONDON

THE MARUZEN-KABUSHIKI-KAISHA
TOKYO, OSAKA, KYOTO, FUKUOKA, SENDAI

THE COMMERCIAL PRESS, LIMITED
SHANGHAI

THE OUTLOOK
FOR AMERICAN PROSE

By

JOSEPH WARREN BEACH

THE UNIVERSITY OF CHICAGO PRESS
CHICAGO · ILLINOIS

Composed and Printed By
The University of Chicago Press
Chicago, Illinois, U.S.A.

NOTE

ESSAYS in this book have appeared in various periodicals, as follows: in *American Speech*, "The Peacock's Tail," "The Naïve Style," and, under the title, "Pedantic Study of Two Critics," those portions of "The Holy Bottle" concerned with Mr. Mencken and Mr. Sherman; in the *Atlantic Monthly*, "Proud Words" and "Sawing the Air"; in the *New Republic*, "English Speech and American Masters"; in the *Virginia Quarterly Review*, that portion of "The Holy Bottle" concerned with Mr. Cabell; in the *Yale Review*, "Unripe Fruits." I wish to acknowledge the courtesy of the editors of the several periodicals in giving permission to reprint these pieces. In some cases the essays have been somewhat revised or enlarged, but for the most part they appear as first printed.

CONTENTS

LAST WORDS BEFORE GOING TO THE PRINTER

LAST WORDS BEFORE GOING TO
THE PRINTER ·

THIS book I call *The Outlook for American Prose* not because I pretend to be a weather prophet, and that I can tell anybody just what to expect in the coming season. It is simply that, in my eagerness to find some development in our prose-writing comparable to what has taken place in our poetry, I have for some time been watching the heavens and considering in myself the meaning of this or that phenomenon. Many of these essays are simply the complaint of a reader impatient of unlovely writing. Others are an expression of satisfaction with writing which is good. I am afraid I shall be thought to use the microscope more than the telescope; and the reader is left to determine for himself just what may be the present outlook for the art in America. My chief anxiety in contemplating these essays in the aggregate is lest my persistent nagging of certain eminent writers may give the impression of an ill-humor which I am far from feeling.

If I were as clever as Mr. Heywood Broun, I should follow the example he sets in one of his most

[3]

entertaining collections of newspaper essays, and write a preface in the form of a review of the book I was offering the public, calling attention to as many as possible of the weak points of the book, and so disarming criticism on these points as far as possible. I should find fault with the author for coming back so often to the same writers; for being so uncertain, or so vacillating, in his opinion upon a given writer; for not knowing just what he thinks, in the end, of the outlook for American prose. And then I should point out the weakness he shows in not allying himself with any particular school of writers, not pinning his faith to any particular type of prose—old-fashioned or new-fashioned. And, finally, I should find fault with him for not being up-to-date, for leaving out of account, in considering several of these writers, their latest published works. Having duly scolded the author for these obvious shortcomings, I should proceed to insinuate an apology for him on each of the counts named.

I should explain that these essays were written at various times, ranging from early in 1921 to the first of January, 1926, and first published in various periodicals at dates suiting the convenience of the editors; and that they are for the most part left in the original form, if only that they may keep, each one, some semblance of the shapeliness I tried to give them. This means that, in certain essays, I make my comment as much on English as on American authors, and that, in many of them, I have failed to include mention of books later in date than those discussed. An essay on Mr. Van Vechten's novels ("The Peacock's Tail"), first written about New Year's, 1924, brought up to date a year later so as to include a view of *The Tattooed Countess*, and published in a magazine in November, 1925, makes no mention of what is, at my present writing, his latest novel, *Firecrackers*. And that is, indeed, an anomaly in an essay considering Mr. Van Vechten as the very high priest of the *dernier cri*. But I prefer to leave the matter so, with the addition of the following note on *Firecrackers* taken from the catalogue of a Philadelphia bookseller: "Mr. Van Vechten still has his same marvelous gift for embellishing a Sears Roebuck catalog with all the rich exuberance of a cross-word puzzle vocabulary, making his scholarly mess more palatable with an occasional old-fashioned drummer's tale." It seems this leopard has not changed his spots. And in any case, the fact of the essay's being now so far from up to date is a quaint ironic comment on the whole subject of literary modes and novelties. It takes a fast runner to keep up with Mr. Van Vechten.

If there are writers to whom I return with unseemly frequency, considering the mean things I have to say of them, it is that they are writers whom I keep on reading in spite of the irritation they cause me as a lover of fine writing; and they are crucial instances of the most besetting problem for anyone trying to make a candid evaluation of American prose. They represent the combination of great merits in general conception and design with a slipshod and often vulgar style of writing. And they make one ask: Can we no longer demand that degree of correctness and refinement in the handling of the language that is the mark of the classics in the English tongue? I should have liked to include in this volume an essay on "New Intentions in the Novel" which appeared in the *North American Review* in August, 1923, in which I have spoken with enthusiasm of the beauty of design in several of Mr. Hergesheimer's novels; and I hope in the future to write more at length of his fine handling, in a half-dozen novels, of the technical problem of the "point of view," in which matter he and Mrs. Wharton are probably the most illustrious disciples in America of that notable technician, Henry James. But the essays in this book are almost altogether confined to questions of style, and the subject of style is forever bringing me back to the peccancies of Mr. Hergesheimer.

Similarly with Mr. Dreiser. Where it is merely a question of style, several books of varying dates are generally sufficient as a basis for gauging the quality of an author, and the references to Mr. Dreiser in "English Speech and American Masters" are to a comparatively small number of his many books. The further consideration of his style in "Auguries" and in "The Naïve Style'" was provoked by the later reading of *A Book about Myself*. But in "The Naïve Style" I speculate on how far the eventual importance of Mr. Dreiser's books may be affected by the inexpertness of his writing, and I allow myself to make a statement on his view of human nature. This essay was kindly read by Mr. Mencken, in a somewhat balder form than that in which it here appears, and Mr. Mencken was good enough to try to set me right. "It seems to me," he writes, "that you have quite missed Dreiser's significance. To say that what he has to say has been said by Maupassant astonishes me. Have you ever read . . . .?" And he referred me to several books in which Dreiser says things which Maupassant has not said. (Be it noted, in passing, that I did not say "Maupassant'"; I said "Balzac and Zola, Maupassant and Gorky, Arthur Schnitzler and Pio Baroja.") Well, I have gone back to Dreiser again and again, and the more I read him the more I am impressed with the bigness and the humanity of him. I begin to be ashamed of approaching this monument with my microscope. I will even say that there are pages in *Jennie Gerhardt* and *Twelve Men* so sweetly and tenderly human and of such grave simplicity of phrasing that they almost suggest the manner in which *Esther Waters* was written, or *Tess of the D'Urbervilles*. What I shall say when I have read *An American Tragedy* I do not know. But the exigencies of the composing-room are too strong for me, and what I may have to say of *An American Tragedy* will remain unwritten, fortunately enough, since this is the fourth time in this book that I have returned to the puzzling subject of Theodore Dreiser. I still find that, on the whole, he writes crudely by any standard I know how to apply. But I expect to go on reading him.

I leave the story in all its nakedness, trusting that the reader will find in my candor and bepuzzlement as much of the genuine critical spirit as if I had been able to say straight off, on a first glance at this colossal writer, that he is one of the immortals, or that he is no good. Moreover, the case is representative enough of the whole problem set by my title. American prose is in the making. One never plunges into the same stream twice. That is the fun of the thing. We have the pleasure of watching the process of something coming into being. If we are not too anxious to be right in our judgments, we need not be anxious at all. Of course we shall have, in the end, an American prose to be proud of. One can never tell the moment when there will emerge works of art that will be decisive. They will, of course, be good work; for no amount of bad work can stand in the light of good work when that once definitely makes its appearance.

And why should I be afraid of candor in that other matter—my want of adherence to any school or tendency? If there is one thing that should be learned from the historical study of literature to which the university man is pledged, it is that there are a myriad ways of doing well. I may have a "hunch" that the typical artistic prose of the coming generation will be more like that of Mr. Sherwood Anderson or Mr. Waldo Frank than like that of Mr. Cabell or Mr. Mencken. It is obvious that Mr. Cabell and Mr. Mencken owe more to the literary traditions of English prose than Mr. Frank and Mr. Anderson. But Mr. Cabell and Mr. Mencken are somewhat more expert in their styles of writing than Mr. Frank and Mr. Anderson are in theirs. And old-fashioned or new-fashioned, what we want is expertness; what we want is something first-rate.

Sometimes the first-rate will be found in writing

neither old-fashioned nor new-fashioned; something that in its unpretentious simplicity slips in between these worrying categories. Such is the best of the writing of our newspaper essayists. In general, they are too smart for my taste, too flippant and complacently ephemeral, and there you feel the pull of their journalistic connection. The writer of this class who promises to stand up the best is perhaps Mr. Strunsky. He does not set out so militantly to amuse or beguile the reader, certainly not to startle and waylay. But he has his own modest fashion of touching the common points of ordinary experience, without insistence of any kind, but with a delicate flavor of irony, a tolerant wisdom and good feeling, which leaves an after-taste in the mouth like China tea. Mr. Morley has chosen for his collection of modern essays a lovely thing of Mr. Strunsky's called "Nocturne," in which the center of interest in his picture of the Night Court is a street-walker who is brought up for trial "once every three months with fair regularity," and who is there confronted, on the other side of the railing, with a group of well-dressed, sympathetic patrician women who have come to the Night Court to "see life." Mr. Strunsky does not turn on any of the tremolo nor any of the savage irony that the subject might seem to call for, nor is there any hint of the

O. Henry in his treatment. And yet in his quiet way he makes the situation very impressive. This girl has come to look forward to these occasions when she is the prisoner at the bar, since they are her only chance to verify with her own eyes the existence of the society women of whom she reads in the Sunday paper, and the clothes and hairdressing art at which she has guessed from certain store windows. And the author concludes gravely with a paradox that must touch the heart of any discerning reader: "On either side of the railing of the prisoners' cage is an audience and a stage. That is why she would look forward to her regular visits to the Night Court. She saw life there." One must certainly admire a writer who can get the effect of style without any of the tricks of style.

But, having regard to the new-fashioned, and the sort of thing that is most likely to make itself felt in the movement that is sure to come—that is already launched—one will have to reckon with Sherwood Anderson, with this man Hemingway, and even perhaps with Gertrude Stein, who may turn out to be the Ezra Pound of the coming movement in prose, considering her influence on writers who come to us in much less questionable shape. Our prose is of course subject to the same influences as our poetry, and these are the influences to which our painting and sculpture and music are subject. We are bound to see in our prose developments of "modernism" parallel to the developments in all the arts.

As for Waldo Frank, perhaps I should not have paired him with Sherwood Anderson, but rather with Paul Rosenfeld, who has so acutely appraised him, good and bad, in his *Men Seen*. Sherwood Anderson represents the tendency to the "naïve," not in the sense in which I use the word in my essay on "The Naïve Style," but in the sense in which it is used of painters, primitives ancient and modern, who simplify in the interest of feeling and design. Gertrude Stein is "naïve," most readers think, to the point of childishness. The tendency of Paul Rosenfeld is just the contrary. His style is not simplified from that of the Victorian prose-writer, but complicated, intensified, knotted up, tangled up, speeded up.

Mr. Rosenfeld is a critic to be reckoned with. He is a sort of follower of Huneker—the introducer of great foreign names in music, painting, letters, and the generous discoverer of American pioneers in all the arts. He writes much better than Huneker, and he has a much sharper mind. His critical essays are original creations in thought and expression, at the same time that they interpret, criticize, and appraise. He has the faculty of making you think you know a composer or a painter whom you have never heard or seen. I have never seen a picture of Marsden Hartley, but I shall recognize without a label the first one I come upon. Do I not know "those great dark pears, bedded upon hospital-white linen on a background of severe dry black"; have I not lived through Hartley's New Mexico in Rosenfeld's description—"with its strange depraved topography . . . . strawberry-pink mountains dotted by fuzzy poison-green shrubs, recalling breasts and wombs of clay; clouds like sky-sailing featherbeds; boneyard aridity"? Mr. Rosenfeld is that rare thing, a critic that approaches a work of art as a work of art; and he has probably succeeded in several dozen essays in avoiding the use of the words "moral" and "realistic." He has the faculty of intensely admiring great talents without losing his head and growing blind to their defects. He can tell you what is the matter with James Joyce without minimizing his greatness. He can find the falsity in a writer without the application of dry, infertile formulas of "humanism" and "naturalism."

He brings to his writing a prodigious imagination, an intensity at once of thought and sensation, an oriental opulence and profusion and bizarrerie. He has all the jargon of the studios, which would be dry stuff did he not water it with deluges of poetical imagery. We may call him a futurist in style. His pages have all the force and rush and confusion of a modern street-scene; they are the literary counterparts of steam engines, skyscrapers, steel mills, electric signs, whirling wheels, and circling searchlights. There is the perpetual flare of Roman candles and the sizz and pop of skyrockets. He uses the English language with the freedom of a caveman using a woman. He stretches our idioms to fit every need of expression, makes it stand on its head, joining words together in strange, illicit unions, and piling metaphor on metaphor. He has no pity.

The Chinese knew themselves *intergrown with* all creation, knew no thing not intergrown with them, and their wisdom symbolized itself in the completeness and harmoniousness, the *balancedness* of their expressions. The great modern Frenchmen saw the world so, and accepted it fully, ugliness and pain and beauty alike, and their wisdom became the *impeccable* organization, the *exquisite* balance that *enthralls* us before the canvases of Cézanne and Renoir. But to this New England work [he is speaking of Marsden Hartley] the same wisdom has not always contributed. The object has in some fashion remained always subordinate to the worker. It has been considered essentially an inferior thing, with the unique function of demonstrating some *ineffable* quality which is *sensed present* in the person regarding far more than in the substance regarded.

To my conservative taste the convenience of such a word as "balancedness" is no excuse for its employment; it is simply too horrid, too impossible to say, and our language is plastic enough to furnish ways of saying the thing without it. As for "sensed present," I recognize the economy and force gained, but there is a point where force and economy must yield to pleasantness of sound and immediate lucidity of meaning. The words "impeccable," "exquisite," "enthralls," and "ineffable" I have italicized because they are words which betray the somewhat forced and factitious character of Mr. Rosenfeld's energy. They are not the most characteristic feature of his writing, but they are characteristic, and they are unpleasantly suggestive of the gush that weakens the work of Huneker and all his kind. The danger of the futurist is not his strength but the forcing of his strength. And there is a strength in quiet reserve as well as in shouting and waving of arms.

I have lingered so over Mr. Rosenfeld because he is not the sole one of his kind, but merely the most brilliant of a kind which is very large in numbers, much larger than the kind represented by Mr. Anderson. This disposition to speed things up, to crowd the palette, to stretch our language to its fullest expressiveness, is to be found in many critics, in writers of fiction, in poets. There was something of it in Amy Lowell, with her *tendre* for hyphenated words of color notation—"Red foxgloves against a

yellow wall streaked with plum-colored shadows"
—with her shrill cries of animal pain—her red slippers, "festooning from the ceiling like stalactites of
blood, flooding the eyes of passers-by with dripping
color, jamming their crimson reflections against the
windows of cabs and tram-cars, screaming their
claret and salmon into the teeth of the sleet"—her
row of white, sparkling shop-fronts that "is gashed
and bleeding, it bleeds red slippers." There is still
more of it in Maxwell Bodenheim, in the degree that
his ideas are more densely crowding, more energetic,
original, and strained. Perhaps the most promising
of the novelists in this movement is Mr. Dos Passos,
who uses this "futurist" style so generally in the
descriptive and narrative passages of *Manhattan
Transfer.*

> Arm and arm they careened up Pearl Street under the
> drenching rain. Bars yawned bright to them at the corners of
> rainseething streets. Yellow light off mirrors and brass rails
> and gilt frames round pictures of pink naked women was looped
> and slopped into whiskeyglasses guzzled fiery with tipped back
> head, oozed bright through the blood, popped bubbly out of
> ears and eyes, dropped spluttering off fingertips. The raindark
> houses heaved on either side, streetlamps swayed like lanterns
> carried in a parade, until Bud was in a back room full of nudg-
> ing faces with a woman on his knees.

I admire Mr. Dos Passos with all my heart, and
as much perhaps for *Manhattan Transfer* as for *Three*

Soldiers. But I think it is less for this feature of his style than for the broader futurism of his method in presenting his material—his blocks of human experience weirdly juxtaposed, his strangely woven strands of fate and impulse. And even more than that I admire him for the material itself—for his amazing knowledge of people and things. Let us hail him at once the indubitable superior of Virginia Woolf, to mention but one of the school of Joyce; her superior—our American author—just as the Irishman is her superior, by the many degrees in which he surpasses her in his knowledge of life. For here is one who "has the goods." But as to his style in the narrower sense, I do not feel so sure. It is competent enough, but I wonder if it does not need moderating, disciplining. With Mr. Rosenfeld I feel more certain that that is what his writing needs.

And yet there is tremendous vigor and promise in this movement, and the future seems to lie between this and the tendency represented by Mr. Anderson. Both will flourish, no doubt, and there will flourish some manner of writing that is the offspring of their union. In Dos Passos, as in Waldo Frank, there are passages that suggest this union not yet quite accomplished. There are points of kinship between the two when compared with an earlier prose. They are both in line with the tendencies in painting, though not with identical tendencies. They are both in line with current psychology, as many of the writers are aware. They make much more of sense impressions and less of intellectual statements and formulations. They prefer the most direct route to the seat of consciousness.

For myself, I do not particularly care what style prevails so long as it is handled with distinguished art. The university man is necessarily an eclectic, and what he asks of writing is that it should be first-rate.

New Year's, 1926

UNRIPE FRUITS

UNRIPE FRUITS

THE OUTLOOK FOR AMERICAN PROSE

WE have had our classical period in American literature—a period largely of cultivated and anemic writers milk fed upon the culture of England. We are at present extremely conscious of the need for a literature more indigenous, more expressive of ourselves, bolder and more original than that of Lowell and Longfellow. In fiction, perhaps, and certainly in poetry, our prayers are being answered, and we have at least a Frost, a Masters, and a Sandburg to offer as the first-fruits of a new age. These are authors representative, distinctively American in flavor, and full of invention in form and style. In prose-writing other than fiction, perhaps in fiction, too, we are at a loss to point out any body of writing comparable to our poetry.

This is normal and to be expected, and does not contradict our hope and faith for a new order in our literature. It is probably true that poetry is the first to flower in any springtime of literary production.

Poetry represents the more instinctive, the more emotional and exclamatory phase of literary expression; prose, the more mature and critical phase. Poetry implies a lively and spontaneous imagination; prose implies a more considerate procedure, a greater saturation with intellectual culture on the part of both writer and reader.

Fiction occupies, we may suppose, an intermediate position. In fiction, even the most thoughtful and sophisticated, the story carries ever the leading rôle; and a story vividly imagined and well told will cover a multitude of shortcomings in thought and expression. I have spoken elsewhere of the frequent stylistic crudenesses and absurdities of current novels, particularly American novels; and in some cases, in spite of these crudities and absurdities in expression, it will be a novelist of considerable distinction, whom one cannot but admire for his invention, his truth to some aspect of life, his story-telling power.

But when it comes to prose of a more philosophic character, the prose of the essay—a prose dedicated to meditation, reminiscence, criticism, social commentary—the matter of style is of infinitely greater importance. I sometimes think it is the great determining factor in the rank of prose-writers. The philosophy of a Carlyle, a Ruskin, a Matthew Arnold, a

Walter Pater, would lose three-fourths of its interest and appeal if delivered in a style less individual, less expert, and less beautifully colored than that of these several writers. And if Emerson is the only American prose-writer of their time worthy to be classed with them and the other great English stylists of the nineteenth century, that is a measure of the comparative poverty of American literature of that century. Havelock Ellis, in his remarkable philosophic study called *The Dance of Life*, quotes some philosopher as saying that Truth is a shade, and he adds on his own account that Beauty is a shade. He means that, while all the great ideas of civilized men are common property—common places as most men phrase them—it is the special turn of the thought given by men of subtlety and originality that makes their power of appeal, that makes them live and mean something. And when it comes to subtlety, that is likely to be developed only in a deep and rich soil of culture, in a society long accustomed to deal with ideas, with sentiments, in a free and natural manner. That implies a settled society; it implies leisure and the disposition to prize highly those intangibles that make the difference between civilization and the raw state of frontier life.

It is only natural that, in this kind of writing, we should find much more numerous examples in a country like England, where they have such long accumulations of the fruits of leisure; where they have been so long depositing and fertilizing the soil of culture. It is much easier to make a list of distinguished prose-writers in contemporary England than in contemporary America. We have produced nothing like the work of Lytton Strachey in his *Eminent Victorians* and *Queen Victoria;* nothing quite like the work of Percy Lubbock in his book on *The Craft of Fiction* or his *Roman Pictures*, though we certainly have reason to rejoice in Mr. Young's *Three Fountains;* no newspaper essayists so witty and high toned as Gilbert Chesterton; nothing in the critical vein so witty and thought-stimulating as the prefaces of Bernard Shaw; no books of reminiscence and natural history so charming as those of W. H. Hudson; no book of family history so civilized as *Our Family Affairs*, by E. F. Benson; no books of travel and foreign impressions so racy and imaginative as those of H. M. Tomlinson and Maurice Hewlett. We did have in philosophy the miraculous case of William James, who wrote literature whatever his subject; and we have a sort of claim on George Santayana, than whom there can be no more humane and gracious and subtle writer on the borderland of philosophy and *belles lettres*. But our claim on him is very slight. He is the product really of

English and Spanish culture; there is no reflection in his work of any of the distinctive color of American thought; and he has appropriately enough gone to spend the rest of his life in the England where he most belongs. He is more English than American; and his chief rivals in the writing of cultivated philosophical prose at the present time are the altogether English Bertrand Russell and Havelock Ellis.

As we look about us at the present time there are several American prosateurs who make a considerable claim to distinction. Sherwood Anderson, in *A Story-Teller's Story*, has produced an autobiography which is at the same time a piece of literary criticism of prime importance; he has a style altogether American, simple, correct, ingenious, and highly original, and a way of presenting his personal history that is a marvel of ingenuity. Mr. Mencken is a critic who never bores you. He is certainly thought provoking; he knows how to write sentences that stand firmly on their feet; he says precisely what he wants to; he says it in good American English and with a vigor and a raciness reminiscent of Swift and Rabelais. His great antagonist in the critical game is Mr. Sherman. He is a judicious and witty writer, who has often taken a fall out of Mencken with his Socratic and jiu-jitsu methods of urbane wrestling. He is a plausible representative of that enlightened Puritanism which is the attitude of so large a body of thoughtful Americans. And then there is Mr. Cabell, who has written two such capital books of criticism in *Beyond Life* and *Straws and Prayer-books*, especially *Beyond Life*. Mr. Cabell brings to the illustration of his romantic theory of literature such intellectual subtlety, such ripened culture, and a style so rich, suave, pointed, and original that he must be counted with assurance as one contemporary American critic who has produced criticism which is literature.

And that is, perhaps, about all we have to show as yet in the way of high distinguished writing in prose not fiction. Of course I do not mean that we have not other writers who handle English prose with correctness, elegance, and authority. One has only to think of the host of university scholars who, in biography, in history, in literary exposition, maintain the very highest standard of good writing short of actual imaginative creation. I am trying to apply the standard set by Dr. Johnson in his *Lives of the Poets*, by Ruskin in his *Stones of Venice*, by Fuller in his *English Worthies*—writers who brought to their work something more peculiarly their own than learning and judgment, and who made of the English language a jewel casket and a shrine. It would be invidious to name, however honorably, the professors of literature in our universities who have set forth some phase of literary history or have helped us to form our opinions on vexed critical problems, but who, with all their knowledge and critical discrimination, will hardly be granted that touch of genius which makes a permanent artistic possession of Lamb's essay *On the Artificial Comedy of the Last Century* or Pater's *The Renaissance*. I am looking for writers so individual in their manner and approach that anyone acquainted with their style could at once identify a new piece of their writing and declare with confidence, "This is Charles Doughty," or "This is Bernard Shaw."

And it is possible that we have writers who would stand this test and whom we find it difficult, even so, to set down as vigorous and characteristic products of present-day American culture. There are doubtless many readers well-enough acquainted with the personal idiosyncrasy and charm of Dr. Crothers or Miss Repplier to be able to recognize them wherever encountered by the special flavor of their work. And it is no doubt a great asset to American letters to have essayists as fine, as subtle, as cultivated, as delicately flavored as Dr. Crothers and Miss Repplier. They are a standing proof that we are capable of culture and refinement, and that the air of America is not everywhere thin and hard to breathe. But can we really persuade ourselves that they are original monuments of American spiritual life? Are they not mainly an evidence of our capacity for assimilation?

SCIENTIFIC JARGON: MR. VAN WYCK BROOKS

If we wish to make a fair appraisal of contemporary American prose, and get a just notion of our prospects for the future, we must take writers more distinctively American, writers more involved in our special problems, who have cut loose from a foreign tradition and are really undertaking to sail new seas. And in general we shall find these forward-looking men to be subject to crudities and stammerings not characteristic of Miss Repplier and our university critics. A typical and significant case is that of Mr. Van Wyck Brooks. He is a writer who is particularly concerned himself with the cultivation in America of what he calls "creative literaature." He enjoys a high and well-deserved consideration among students of American literature because of his studies of Mark Twain and Henry James. And he has written more than one book on the general situation in America. In *Letters and Leadership*, Mr. Brooks complains that we do not have creative literature in America because all our energies have been directed to the material development of the country. Our critics, he says, have joined in the conspiracy to discourage any free use of the creative impulses because they were felt to be at war with the possessive impulses which must be given the right of way. Puritanism has joined with industrialism to choke out artistic expression.

Now that is a very plausible hypothesis, and one with which half our present-day critics agree. But the discouraging thing about Mr. Brooks is that, with all his desire to foster the imaginative life, he cannot seem to free himself—at least in his program-book—from the very materialism which he deplores. His style is, throughout, the style of a scientific and industrial age. To all that he writes there clings what Mr. T. S. Eliot calls, in another connection, "that familiar vague suggestion of scientific vocabulary which is characteristic of modern writing." The very terms in which he pictures the spiritual aims of our more promising writers are taken from the most material of sciences, dynamics, and the most utilitarian, industrial economics. These men, he says, are struggling "for a world that is able to keep and use the whole of its creative energy." He proposes for American art "a programme for the conservation of our spiritual resources." He would like to cultivate national ideals "by virtue of which the springs of our creative energy are not only touched into play but so econo-mized as to be able to irrigate the entire subsoil of our national life." He takes Goethe's phrase for the right poetic approach to life, "from within out-wards," and renders it in this same lingo of dynam-ics and industrial economics: "It is the effective approach because it envisages method in terms of value, every ounce of pressure that is put upon value registering itself with a tenfold intensity, so to speak, in the sphere of application." Again, upon figures from dynamics, he is fond of grafting figures taken vaguely from architecture, producing, I should say, a very dubious hybrid. "As soon as the founda-tions of our life have been reconstructed and made solid on the basis of an experience of which we have shown the potentialities, all these extraneous, ill-regulated forces will rally about this new-found cen-ter; they will fit in, each where it belongs, con-tributing to the essential architecture of our life." The general effect of this program is not less dismal for the fact that the figures are mixed, and that forces and potentialities are shown now rallying round a center, now fitting into a framework, and now contributing to an architecture.

It will be remarked that Mr. Brooks does not in general draw from the arts and sciences concrete imagery which will really brighten and illustrate his subject; but that his comparisons serve only to make the subject more abstract and theoretical than it was to start with. This is not the architecture from which Lamb borrowed his figure for ears, "hanging ornaments, and (architecturally speaking) handsome volutes to the human capital," not that decorative and eye-pleasing aspect of the building art, but an aspect at the same time utilitarian and abstract, practical and theoretical. "Essential architecture" indeed! Essential architecture is geometry, and metaphysical geometry at that. Circles and triangles may be the stuff of "creative literature," of poetry and religion. Essential architecture belongs to a fashion of thought, to use one of Mr. Brooks's brighter phrases, "so denatured, so stripped of everything that might nourish the imagination," that we cannot well associate it with the workings of the "creative mind."

The most arid and withering of the provinces from which we derive imagery in these days is the province of psychology. And Mr. Brooks has duly built into his architecture many dry branches from the *hortus siccus* of psychological jargon. We have a great deal about "people who externalize themselves in a world of externalities," of that "complicated scheme of ideal objectives" which we must secure in America before we can hope to build up a civilization. We read that the matter with Dr. Crothers as a prophet of culture is that

while the self-consciousness of the younger generation stands for an instinctive drive toward a common understanding on the creative plane, the self-consciousness of Dr. Crothers, making no levy upon our creative life, accepts the pioneer law of self-preservation, in the scheme of which literature is only a kind of associational and secondary play of the mind in a society whose real business is the art of getting on.

There is something about the syntax of that sentence that suggests the influence of Matthew Arnold, who did for Victorian England what Mr. Brooks is undertaking to do for present-day America. But this only serves to remind us that Matthew Arnold deliberately "laboured to divest knowledge of all that was harsh, uncouth, difficult, abstract, professional, exclusive"; that he did not draw his words and images from the abstract realms of science but took them bright and sharp from everyday experience— "sweetness and light, doing as one likes, Barbarians and Philistines, reason and the will of God." Mr. Brooks need not expect that "creative literature" can be synthetically produced in any laboratory; or that she is sired, as Mr. Mencken would say, by psychology out of physics. She is, I shrewdly suspect, the daughter of "heart-easing Mirth," and *she* is, as everybody knows, either the daughter of Venus and Bacchus or else of Zephyr and Aurora.

UNRIPE FRUITS

I think the reader will agree that there is little sap or savor in writing like this, however right the author may be in his theory about American literature. This is, I rejoice to say, not characteristic of Mr. Brooks at his best; but it is characteristic enough of the average writing in our weekly journals, from which Mr. Brooks has taken his spring into deeper waters. And this at least makes sense; it has a core of solid truth. There are men who have won much greater popularity by writing which, in its emptiness, its parade of rubber-stamp phrases which are meant to take the place of ideas, can be the source of little but boredom for readers who demand either intellectual or imaginative stimulus. Examples of this style are not far to seek, but I take mine from an author of sufficient distinction to give point to their citation. These passages are from what were originally public addresses, but they were thought important enough to be given the permanency of cold print and a bound volume. If the book is now several years old, that will make it the easier to recognize the true quality of these phrases; for in the heat of the moment we are as prone as the speaker himself to be taken in by the verbal coin of the moment. This is an author who manages to express his opinion on almost every sub-

[33]

ject of public interest at the time of his lectures
without danger of offending any person of an opposite opinion, since he takes a position in every case
such that he agrees with all parties to a dispute.

This, for example, is the high and safe line he
takes in regard to the economic problems of our
time:

> Labor and capital must join in a high resolve that both
> shall strive, in consonance with the spirit of peace and toler-
> ance, to think less in terms of the battlefield and more in terms
> of the council-chamber. The battle mind has been inevitable
> in the labor-capital struggles of the past, but pure tests of
> strength, such as bargainings and strikes, can never bring in-
> dustrial health to the world. Nothing save some continuously
> just administration of industry can do that. Such administra-
> tion can never come as the by-product of a fight. It must be the
> consciously conceived product of industrial statesmanship, and
> industrial statesmanship is impossible without the spirit of
> tolerant good-will and mutual respect.

There is nothing here that could give offense to
either employer or employee. It is safe enough for
the utterance of a United States senator.

Hear him now on a political theme:

> If there ever was a time in American history when the need
> for setting up the instruments and methods for common discus-
> sion of common interests was imperative, it is now in this time
> of flux, when reckless revolution and stupid reaction are alike
> coquetting with the public mind, making balanced sanity of
> mass judgment increasingly difficult. . . . . It is not enough
> merely to put our fingers to our ears when false guides speak;

the task remains of producing national policies that will go between and beyond the caveman politics of the Bourbon and the Cubist politics of the Bolshevist. It would seem a waste of words to say that, in the sort of time we are passing through, nothing will so surely protect us from hasty experiment and insure rational progress as the full, free, candid, serious, and sustained discussion, etc. . . . . We must somehow contrive to have the clean and antiseptic air of free discussion blow through the recesses of our national thought.

You get the characteristic flavor better still if you leave out the connecting thought and string along in sequence the mustier and more shopworn of the phrases: "If there ever was a time when . . . . need was imperative . . . . this time of flux . . . . reckless revolution. . . . . It is not enough merely. . . . . It would seem a waste of words to say . . . . the clean and antiseptic air of free discussion." Best of all, the phrase occurring in other passages, the phrase of the man who is infallibly going to say something of no importance, "I cannot, somehow, help thinking. . . . ."

Hear him on the subject of Americanization:

No straight-thinking person disputes the need of a fundamentally sound program of Americanization, a vast collective effort toward the stimulation and spread of sane principles of national life among all sorts and conditions of men and women who make up our population. But anything and everything that goes by the name of Americanization is not necessarily an effective move in that direction. There is slowly growing up a body of incisive criticism dealing with the current epidemic of Americanization work that is sweeping the country on the wings of clever catchwords and generous emotions.

I do not for a moment think of disputing the author's contention in this case. Only I do wish he would spare me his "straight-thinking person," his "fundamentally sound program," his "sane principles of national life." In so far as they are generous emotions I agree; in so far as they are clever catchwords I ask for a truce.

The reader is doubtless disappointed and surprised that I have not yet brought in "dynamic conceptions" or "constructive conservatism." It is only for lack of time that I do not quote the passage on "The Lawyer as Leader" in which these consecrated phrases appear in force. But no lack of time can prevent me from quoting this energetic and alliterative utterance on the educational problem of the moment:

> The present stage of our progress of educational redefinition is marked by our attempt to shake off the dangerous dominance of the specialist who has done the double damage to our educational system of dehumanizing it and of splitting our curricula into airtight compartments of unrelated knowledge.

Ah well! we are all miserable sinners. Who among us has not dealt frequently in "airtight compartments"? Let him that is guiltless among us cast the first stone!

A friend of mine to whom I read some of these passages—a shrewd lawyer and a man who never employs this style himself—remarked, "But this is no worse than any public speaker." Well, thinks I, that is just it. That is, I suspect, what is the matter with American political thought. And that is, I am sure, what is the matter with American prose. If Mr. Brooks's style in *Letters and Leadership* is the style of our weekly journals at their average, the style of this publicist is that of these weekly journals at their worst. On the average, they are saying fairly important things in a manner superficially smart but in the long run rather dreary; at their worst, they are covering a vague liberalism with empty phrases.

INCOHERENCE IN THE AESTHETE: MR. JOSEPH HERGESHEIMER

But there are other literary vices almost as serious as dreariness and emptiness, and quite as widespread among our representative prosateurs. There is what the rhetoricians call "incoherence," and for examples of that I turn to writers very much better known than either of these referred to. I turn to the famous novelist, Mr. Joseph Hergesheimer, and the famous philosopher, Mr. John Dewey. It is in his book about Cuba, *San Cristóbal de la Habana*, that Mr. Hergesheimer has entered the ranks of writers of thoughtful prose. Here, without story, he under-takes to render the feeling and atmosphere of the Spanish-American city of Cuba and especially his own impressions of Havana. And he goes about the matter with the finical elaborateness of self-analysis of Henry James in *The American Scene* or *Notes of a Son and Brother.* The difficulty is that what in James are mannerisms reflecting his original bent and serving his purpose become in Hergesheimer simple affectations. James is fussy, if you will; Her-gesheimer is fussy and ostentatious, fussy and often unintelligible. James is a model of moderation in emphasis; Hergesheimer underlines every other phrase. The sentences of James are always lucid enough and carrying a precise meaning, however complicated and wiredrawn it may be, and the values are artfully distributed and in accordance with good English usage. In Hergesheimer the word order is often forced and constantly serves to lead the reader astray as to the meaning or the shade of meaning. Every page makes me knit my brows, and relief comes only with the inevitable "howler," the statement so Hibernian in its unintended humor that perplexity gives way to mirth. Thus when Mr. Hergesheimer is speaking of the pleasure he took in a Cuban opera company he had heard in New York. "But not so much for the singing," he says, "it had been the dancer, Doloretes, who captivated me, a woman as brilliant as the orange-red shawl draped before me over a chair, and suddenly, tragically, dead in New York." It took me an appreciable interval to correct my impression that it was the red shawl that died in New York, and that was enough to disperse altogether the sense of tragedy in the death of the lady who captivated Mr. Hergesheimer. In speaking of gardenias, he says, "A curious flower, I thought, getting water for them in a glass. They didn't wilt, as was usual, but turned brown and faded in the manner of a lovely pallid woman—a simile I had used in Linda Condon." I had to reflect for some time before I made out why these flowers did not wilt as was usual; until at last I realized that he did not mean, "They didn't wilt, as was usual," but "They didn't wilt like other flowers," or "as it is usual for flowers to wilt." Being gardenias they stood up. In speaking of the different impressions he had of Cuban and New York hotels, Mr. Hergesheimer says, "For myself, my entire attitude was different in the room I now inhabited from the inherent feeling, in New York, of the Algonquin." This sentence I did not find it actually hard to understand. I knew at once that Mr. Hergesheimer meant that he felt different in the Havana hotel from what he did in the New York hotel. But

I could not help making a wry face when he compared his attitude in Cuba with the feeling of the hotel in New York; and when he talks of the "inherent feeling" of the New York hotel, it takes me a moment to realize that he means nothing at all, but that he is simply flirting with a word that strikes him as pretty.

But I have so often paid my respects to Mr. Hergesheimer that I will now confine myself to the quotation of one somewhat longer passage from his book on Havana by way of suggesting the difficulties he makes for the reader who wishes to follow him through the length of a paragraph. Something has suggested to him the aristocratic luxuriousness of yachts, and he goes on to say:

I had always liked worldly pomp and settings, marble Georgian houses. . . . . I'd rather be on a yacht than on an excursion boat; yet I infinitely preferred reading about the latter. For some hidden or half-perceived reason, yachts were not impressive in creative prose; there the concerns and pleasures of aristocracy frequently appeared tawdry and unimportant. Even its heroism, in the valor of battle and imperturbable sacrifice, was less moving to me than simpler affairs. Yet there was no doubt but that I was personally inclined to the extremes of luxury; and this apparent contradiction brought to my life, my writing, the problem of a devotion to words as disarmingly simple as the leaves of spring—as simple and as lovely in clear color—about the common experience of life and death, together with an absorbing attention for Manchu women and exotic children and emeralds.

[40]

Now I have, I think, worked out the meaning of this paragraph. Mr. Hergesheimer means to say that, while personally he likes yachts for their aristocratic character, he has found mere democratic excursion boats better subjects for literature; and that, paradoxically, while he prefers very homely words in his writing, he is fascinated by themes anything but homely. It is the last sentence that gives the most trouble. Was it his devotion to words that was so disarmingly simple, as one first supposes, or was it that he was devoted to words that are disarmingly simple? As for his "absorbing attention for Manchu women,'" we can only let that go as a new invention in English idiom. He does not mean that he was very attentive to Manchu women, but simply that they constituted a subject that captivated his attention.

INCOHERENCE IN THE PHILOSOPHER: MR. JOHN DEWEY

Half of the absurdities of Mr. Hergesheimer arise from affectation working hand in hand with carelessness. He affects the careless manner of a cultivated gentleman and expert in writing, a sort of Lord Byron of prose, improvising his oriental tales while making his toilet before his looking-glass. Different as is Professor Dewey—worlds distant from Mr.

Hergesheimer in subject matter and tone—yet there is here, too, I suspect a certain pride of carelessness. Mr. Dewey is the champion of the natural and instinctive as against the pedantic and the formally logical in thought and conduct. And there may be some connection between his general attitude toward life and thought and the carelessness which often makes him such hard reading. I am greatly in sympathy with many of the opinions of Mr. Dewey, and I recognize his very great reputation among American philosophers. But his extreme want of precision in writing makes me uneasy—it makes me wonder if there is something unsound about his thinking. If that is so, his eminence among American thinkers, the readiness with which he is generally accepted as a profound thinker, would be a measure of what we lack in the way of critical culture.

As an example of Mr. Dewey's writing, I shall cite a somewhat lengthy passage taken from his interesting book on *Human Nature and Conduct*. It is from the first chapter, in which Mr. Dewey is setting forth the idea that standards in conduct are the product of social conditions, and particularly that rules of conduct, codes of morality, are often the means by which the ruling caste enforces its own will upon the subject castes and thereby establishes its supremacy. Mr. Dewey goes on to point out the need for a scientific study of human nature if we are to have a proper understanding of such rules of conduct. I shall first quote as it stands one continuous passage in which he develops this phase of the theme. I shall then offer a new rendering of the passage, including such changes as are necessary to make the author's meaning intelligible to the ordinary reader, putting in italics those sentences or phrases which represent a radical alteration of the original or which have been supplied for the sake of clearness. And then I shall go on to analyze a few sentences of the original in order to show the complicated process of reconstruction which it is necessary for any reader to go through in order to arrive at the author's meaning. If it is objected that this is nothing more nor less than a pedantic re-writing of a theme such as is proper in college classes in composition, I can only say that that is precisely my business in life and the way in which I justify my existence in so far as I do so at all.

Here, then, is the passage from Mr. Dewey:

But no matter how much men in authority have turned moral rules into an agency of class supremacy, any theory which attributes the origin of rule to deliberate design is false. To take advantage of conditions after they have come into existence is one thing; to create them for the sake of an advantage to accrue is quite another thing. We must go back to the bare fact of social division into superior and inferior. To say that accident produced social conditions is to perceive that they were not produced by intelligence. Lack of understanding of human nature is the primary cause of disregard for it. Lack of insight always ends in despising or else unreasoned admiration. When men had no scientific knowledge of physical nature they either passively submitted to it or sought to control it magically. What cannot be understood cannot be managed intelligently. It has to be forced into subjection from without. The opaqueness of human nature to reason is equivalent to a belief in its irregularity. Hence a decline in the authority of social oligarchy was accompanied by a rise of scientific interest in human nature. This means that the make-up and working of human forces afford a basis for moral ideas and ideals. Our science of human nature in comparison with physical sciences is rudimentary, and morals which are concerned with the health, efficiency and happiness of a development of human nature are correspondingly elementary. These pages are a discussion of some phases of the ethical change involved in positive respect for human nature when the latter is associated with scientific knowledge.

Now let us try to put into clear and coherent terms what Professor Dewey seems to mean:

But no matter how much men in authority have turned moral rules into an agency of class supremacy, *it would be a mistake to suppose that these rules were created originally with the* deliberate design *of using them for this purpose.* It is one thing to take advantage of conditions after they have come into existence; it is quite another thing to create them for the sake of an advantage to accrue. *To understand a system of morals,* we must go back to the division into classes,—into superior and inferior. *We shall find that social conditions grew up spontaneously, and that*

*is as much as to say that they were not the product of deliberate thought.
Just the contrary, they were the product of a want of intelligence in
interpreting human nature. Human nature was disregarded in framing moral rules because it was not understood.* Lack of insight *into
anything* leads to its being despised or else admired unreason-
ably. *It is so with* physical nature; when men had no knowledge
of it, they either passively submitted to it or sought to control
it magically. What cannot be understood cannot be managed
intelligently. It has to be forced into subjection from without.
In the case of human nature, *the difficulty of understanding it leads
to the assumption that it is essentially arbitrary in its action, only
to be controlled from without. This is the assumption of all social
oligarchy, and it is an assumption which social oligarchy finds it to
its advantage to maintain. And this in turn prevents the growth of
any scientific study of human nature. But* a decline in the authority
of social oligarchy is *naturally* accompanied by the rise of *that*
scientific interest in human nature *to which social oligarchy has
been opposed. The scientific assumption is that the principles of
morality should be sought in the very constitution of human nature,
and based on a study of* the make-up and *actual* working of human
forces. *It must be acknowledged that*, in comparison with the
physical sciences, our science of human nature is rudimentary,
and morals—*which are concerned with the development of human nature into something* healthful, efficient, and happy—are correspondingly elementary. These pages *will be taken up with* a discussion of some phases of the ethical change involved in *that*
respect for human nature *which results from its being studied in
connection* with scientific knowledge *in general.*

It would be too long an undertaking to explain
the necessity of the several dozen changes made in
order that the course of this thought may be clear
to the reader, if indeed I have succeeded in making

it clear. But it would be worth our while to analyze, through several sentences, the process of trial and error, of guess and reconstruction, in which the reader must at every point engage in order to make any connected sense. Let us begin with the sentence a little below the middle of the passage, "The opaqueness of human nature to reason is equivalent to a belief in its intrinsic irregularity." The first thing the reader does instinctively is to get rid of the words "equivalent to." No fact about human nature is equivalent to any belief about it. Facts are one thing, beliefs another. The general connection makes the reader understand that the author means to say, "The opaqueness of human nature to reason leads to a belief in its intrinsic irregularity." The reader then approaches the phrase, "the opaqueness of human nature to reason." He first translates the figurative phrase into one more consistent with English idiom, and has "the imperviousness of human nature to reason." He supposes it to mean the fact that human nature is dense and irrational, that reason cannot penetrate into it. And so he reads, for simplification, "The irrationality of human nature leads to a belief in its intrinsic irregularity." But that, in the particular connection, makes no sense, and the reader tries again. He takes his cue from the statement two sentences back that what cannot be understood cannot be managed intelligently. Perhaps the author means, not the imperviousness of human nature to reason in the abstract, the irrationality of human nature, but its imperviousness to the understanding of the observer—the difficulty of understanding it. So he tries that. "The difficulty of understanding human nature leads to a belief in its intrinsic irregularity." That does make sense in the connection, providing one develops a little the connotations of the word "irregularity." A thing that is irregular is arbitrary in its action, not to be controlled by reference to its own laws, but only to be forced into subjection from without. So the reader puts the sentence into a form that will suggest that connection, and he proceeds to the following sentence: "The difficulty of understanding human nature leads to an assumption that it is essentially irregular, or arbitrary, in its action. Hence a decline in the authority of social oligarchy was accompanied by a rise of scientific interest in human nature."

Here the reader is plunged into very great difficulties by the use of the logical connective "hence." He does not yet know that Mr. Dewey is particularly cavalier in the use of just this category of words which imply the strictest of logical bonds—that when he uses "in short" very likely he is not summing up the points already made but proceeding to add a new one; that when he says "therefore" he may be meaning "on the other hand." And so the reader takes the word "hence" in its strict sense, and tries to understand how it can be that "since the difficulty of understanding human nature leads to the assumption that it is arbitrary in its action, therefore the decline in the authority of social oligarchy was accompanied by a rise of scientific interest in human nature." He understands the contention that it is the social oligarchs who fail to understand human nature and who, assuming that it is arbitrary in its action, find that they can control it only by forcing it into subjection from without. He can also understand how a rise in scientific interest in human nature would result in a better understanding of it and would consequently undermine the authority of the social oligarchs. But he cannot see that the decline in the authority of the oligarchs would be accompanied by a spontaneous rise of scientific interest in human nature. It must be that some step in the chain of reasoning has been omitted. Perhaps Mr. Dewey means to say that the social oligarchs, finding it to their personal advantage to maintain the supposition that human nature is essentially arbitrary, instinctively discourage the rise of scientific interest in human nature for fear that it will undermine their prestige, and that consequently the rise of scientific interest in human nature is delayed until, through other causes, their authority begins to decline. In that case the missing link will have to be supplied by the reader.

The difficulty of understanding human nature leads to the assumption that it is essentially arbitrary in its action, only to be controlled by being forced into subjection from without. This is the assumption of all social oligarchy, and it is an assumption which social oligarchy finds it to its own advantage to maintain. And this in turn prevents the growth of any scientific study of human nature. But the decline in the authority of social oligarchy was naturally accompanied by the rise of that scientific interest in human nature to which the social oligarchy had been opposed.

Now I do not guarantee that I have correctly rendered the thought of Mr. Dewey, nor even that what I have made of his passage is logical and consistent with itself. But I know that I have done the best I could, the best that a careful and diligent study of his writing makes possible. And I do not think that the difficulty lies in the subject matter, that Mr. Dewey is hard to read because he deals in difficult and abstruse matters. In general, the points he has to make are comparatively simple ones. But my impression is that he has not always thought them out to a clear issue, and still less has he taken pains to put them in terms that will make them clear to his reader.

I·am not at present concerned with the lack of elegance that everywhere characterizes the writing of Mr. Dewey. It may be said that he is dealing with matters of practical importance, and that he has not time to concern himself with the luxuries and refinements of artistic writing. What I am considering is a lack of clearness, a lack of precision; and this looks in two directions. It makes hard reading; that is the rhetorical side of the matter. And I fear that it often implies confusion in the thought; and that looks back to the logical side of the matter, and tends to make us skeptical even as to the soundness and validity of his argument. It may be the pedantry of a student of rhetoric; but I cannot help suspecting that a writer who is constantly guilty of looseness in expression in detail may be sometimes guilty of looseness of thinking in the large.

It would take a long time for me to justify my statement that Mr. Dewey is constantly guilty of looseness in expression, but I will give an example or two of his want of precision in the use of synonyms. The word "quality" and the word "trait" are not words of such vague and all-inclusive meaning as many people seem to suppose; and it is evidence of unnecessary indolence of mind to use them to cover all the meanings of character, capacity, feature, circumstance, habit, faculty, etc., which

Mr. Dewey does use them to cover. "The only way
to achieve *traits* of carefulness," writes Mr. Dewey
in *How We Think,* "The only way to achieve *traits*
of carefulness, thoroughness, and continuity (traits
that are, as we have seen, the elements of the 'logical') is by exercising these *traits* from the beginning." He means presumably, "The only way to
acquire *habits* of carefulness, etc.," and "exercising
these *faculties*." In another more extensive passage
in the same book he uses "qualities" and "traits"
interchangeably to designate the features, the facts,
items, or circumstances connected with a certain
boat by which one arrives at the conclusion that a
certain object on the boat is or is not a flagpole.

Suppose we symbolize the *qualities* that suggest *flagpole* by
the letters a, b, c; those that oppose this suggestion by the letters p, q, r. There is, of course, nothing inconsistent in the
qualities themselves; but in pulling the mind to different and in-
congruous conclusions they conflict—hence the problem. Here
the object is the discovery of some object (O), of which a, b, c,
and p, q, r, may all be appropriate *traits*—just as, in our first
case, it is to discover a course of action which will combine
existing conditions and a remoter result in a single whole. The
method of solution is also the same; discovery of intermediate
qualities (the position of the pilot house, of the pole, the need
of an index to the boat's direction) symbolized by d, g, l, o,
which bind together otherwise incompatible *traits*.

Now these passages, typical of Mr. Dewey's way
of writing in general, are taken from his elementary

treatise, *How We Think*, a manual widely used in classes in education and logic. They represent the carefully considered writing of an educational expert, of a recognized authority on logic, a leader of the American intelligentsia. He is a writer whose work is eagerly accepted by our most influential weekly reviews, and I think he may be taken as representative of American prose-writing of a serious character. The average untrained writer cannot surely be expected to do better than this scholar appointed to the highest posts in several of our greatest universities. As Chaucer has it, "And if gold rust, what shall iron do?" And so we have a plain indication of one of the reasons for the inferiority of American prose-writing to that of England or France. It is a simple lack of intellectual discipline.

NATIONAL TRAITS

Intellectual discipline we have neglected because we have no time for it, or will not give ourselves time. We have still in our nerves the strain of effort required of our ancestors who undertook to subjugate a continent—the habits of haste and strenuous attack which they had to form if they were to survive and bend to their use the manifold forces of the new world. We have not yet acquired the habit of leisure and of patience to wait upon the slow processes of nature. The typewriter and the short-hand notebook are the symbols of our spiritual state. We insist upon quick returns and those of a kind to fill the eye. We have neither conceived that art is long, nor that in art, as in life, the best things are often the simplest, the homeliest, the least showy. In one way or another, the crudeness of our prose-writing is attributable to our national impatience, our disposition to assume a degree of culture which we do not possess, or to force its development more rapidly than is compatible with soundness and sweetness. Our intellectuals are like coachers standing on the side lines and urging us to steal a base. They seem to think that the shortcomings of American literature may all be laid at the door of puritan Philistinism, overlooking the simple factors of time and ripeness. Our public men confide their voices to electrical amplifiers, trusting that somehow the same machinery that enlarges their words will fill them with substance of thought and personal grace. Their spacious phrases make one think of the false fronts of tin and wood with which railway hotels give themselves importance in Manitoba and Nebraska. Our aesthetes and professors of sensual culture switch on the pink lights; they burn pastilles, and lounging on their plush divans, lispingly recommend their substitutes as cheaper and more satisfying than the genuine article. Our philosophers and pedagogical experts show us a shortcut to right thinking. By example, if not by precept, they assure us that we may "skip" the discipline of rhetoric and proceed at once to the delights of logic and metaphysics. And they encourage us to "reconstruct" philosophy before we have quite assimilated the thought of Plato, Kant, and Descartes.

And we cannot hold our leaders much to blame for conditions which they did not create. In most cases they "get away with" what they undertake; they readily "sell" their gospels to a public hungering and thirsting after culture, and easily satisfied with substitutes. We should be less easily satisfied with substitutes if we insisted on taking pleasure in the process of being cultivated. But in matters of culture we consent to be teased and bored because we trust to be the better for it. We are at the same time too much in a hurry and too anxious. In matters of culture we try too hard and do not leave enough to nature. Of course we have to prepare the soil and water the plants. But we do not want to fuss around the plants too much. Anxiety and self-consciousness are bad for culture. A watched kettle never boils.

ANXIETY: MR. GAMALIEL BRADFORD

A notable example of our anxiety is the writing of Mr. Gamaliel Bradford. We are rightly grateful

to Mr. Bradford for his many and interesting studies
of the souls of notable men and women. Mr. Bradford has many qualifications for his task. He has
patience, industry, sympathy, fairness, subtlety, a
sense of form. He has had one real inspiration in the
title of his *Damaged Souls*. He writes well, and very
well; and it is perhaps ungracious to note that he
does not often write supremely well. He writes well
when he will let himself go. There is, for example,
the inimitable opening paragraph of his chapter on
General Butler:

And still I am looking for a real, live rascal, one who
knows and confesses himself to be such, and boasts of it, who
does not dodge and shift and palter and whip the devil around
the stump, to whom principle is nothing, conscience is nothing, God is nothing, and self and pleasure and success are all.
If I could find him, he should have first place among these
palely damaged, but not completely damned souls. I have not
found him yet and he is certainly not General Benjamin Frank-
lin Butler.

The trouble is that Mr. Bradford, with his New
England nerves all taut, will seldom let himself go.
He takes his task so seriously, and he always lets
us know how seriously he takes it. In 1916 he tells
us of his *Portraits of Women:*

The nine portraits contained in this volume are preliminary
studies or sketches for the series of portraits of American
women which will follow my Union portraits. Such a collection of portraits of women *will certainly fill a most important*

section in the gallery of historical likenesses selected from the whole of American history, which it is my wish to complete, if possible.

In 1922 he tells us, of his *American Portraits*, "This group of portraits is the first of a series *in which I hope to cover American history*, proceeding backwards with four volumes on the nineteenth century, two on the eighteenth, and one on the seventeenth," and he goes on to set forth at length the difficulties he must encounter in performing this task fully and fairly. In 1924 he explains that "*The Soul of Samuel Pepys* and *Bare Souls* represent a digression from the extensive series of American portraits to which *I mean in future to devote all my time and energy*." It is all very well for the student to propose to cover American history and to assure himself that a given collection of portraits will fill a most important section in a gallery which he wishes to complete. But the reader cares for the product and not the labor, and the well-advised author will do away with all traces of the reading-lamp and the green shade of the student.

One of the difficulties of the follower of this "psychographic method"—God save the mark!—is to present every aspect of the soul under investigation and yet to spare us the intolerable burden of scholarly detail. And Mr. Bradford has shown, in-

deed, great courage in his eliminations, great skill in
reducing his enormous material to the compass of an
essay. There are often left, however, traces of this
labor of condensation. We have too much the sense
of the student passing constantly from one topic to
another in a carefully outlined progression. One is
bothered by the clocklike recurrence of formal transitional phrases, as in the essay on Madame de
Sévigné:

> Let us trace further the charming many-sidedness. . . . .
> Yet though she could make. . . . . Yet though she had many
> friends . . . . it must not be supposed. . . . . Nevertheless, it
> would be wholly unjust. . . . . The fact is. . . . . Yet she
> makes the best. . . . . It will naturally be asked. . . . . She
> has her moments, also. . . . . So we have seen Madame de
> Sévigné to be. . . . . For the most part, however, ... But
> it makes no difference. In spite of. . . . . Thus you see, this
> sweet and noble lady. . . . .

Such rhetorical devices, though an evidence of
rhetorical expertness, are at the same time a betrayal of the fact that the author has not achieved
that final synthesis and crystallization of his subject
matter which is demanded of a good portraitist, and
which we recognize with joy in the English gallery
of *Eminent Victorians*. They are an evidence of care
and pains, but not of that final joyous simplification
which is the fruit of leisure and saturation.

Mr. Bradford makes for himself another difficulty
which Mr. Strachey has shed with a shrug of the

shoulders—that of judging his characters as well as presenting them. Mr. Strachey is content to be a portraitist pure and simple. He does not even let us know that he is interpreting, as Mr. Bradford does on every page; and if we feel that he is fair to his characters, it is not because he tells us so. Mr. Bradford, in presenting Mark Twain, feels called upon gravely to consider the question whether that writer for the man in the street did more harm than good, and whether the world was made wholly better by his presence. Even where he is most liberal and indulgent in his interpretation, he seems to have an eye on an audience of censorious puritans. Thus Roosevelt's abhorrence of Thomas Paine, whom he called a "filthy little atheist," stirs Mr. Bradford to a defense which is a credit to his open-mindedness, but which would be superfluous and a little quaint in Mr. Lytton Strachey writing for Mr. Strachey's audience:

No doubt it is good to be clean and sober and conservative and do what your fathers did and shun ideals. But some of us occasionally like to think new thoughts and step out of the beaten track, and we like one who makes us do these things, even if he is a trifle untidy in his person. Here is a man who upset the world and you say that he did not brush his clothes. Here is a man who beat and shook conventions, who stirred up dusty and old titles, till he showed their rotten vanity, and you complain because some of the dust got on himself. This is childishness.

This is very good writing indeed, and the best thing in his essay on Paine. But there is in it a note of nervousness and the consciousness of a daring greater than the subject calls for. And in all of Mr. Bradford's writing we have a sense of a labor and responsibility that rather weighs upon us.

HOPEFUL SIGNS

From Mr. Bradford we turn with a kind of relief to our Simeon Strunskys and our Christopher Morleys, newspaper writers as they are, or have been, finding in their lightness of touch a greater promise for the art we cherish. They travel light, but they travel far. And we likewise discover hope in the direction taken by Rockwell Kent, whose text, starting as the modest accompaniment to his drawings, bids fair to take precedence over them in distinction, rendering so casually the graciousness, the daring, and the broad humanity of the artist's spirit, and with so little circumstance of literary show putting us in touch with the tragedies and wonders of remote places. If only Mr. Kent would rid himself of his habit of writing in blank verse, we should begin to back him as a master of English prose.

But with most conviction we turn again to the author of *A Story-Teller's Story* and the author of *Beyond Life* as showing the way. Mr. Anderson and Mr. Cabell give the impression, more than any of our writers, of men who have taken their time, who have drawn apart from the hurry and distraction of our journalistic life. The one has pondered long in his secluded study on the great imaginative creations of European culture, taking them with a lingering relish. The other has pondered equally, sitting on a Winesburg doorstep or in the front window of his New York rooming-house, on the moving forces of human nature, considering how best on the screen of fiction to project the luminous shades of men and women. In each case the author's approach to his subject is leisurely, often devious and indirect; he approaches it over and over again from different directions, as one approaches a lovely village in Touraine or Tuscany, surveying it from far off and from near by, from every angle and in every phase of sun and moon. He does not attempt to take it by violence; and you are hardly conscious of the moment when he and you seem to have come into possession of it. But in the end you know that you are breathing the air of this fine romantic place—this world-old theory of art, this new-discovered process and technique. You are not so much in possession of it as possessed by it. So it is with any culture worth the name; and such is the hope and promise for American prose. But now, for the most part, the Kingdom of Heaven suffereth violence, and the violent take it by force. MAY, 1925

THE HOLY BOTTLE

THE HOLY BOTTLE

WHAT American prose most lacks is flavor. Too often it lacks precision as well, but not so often as it lacks flavor. Among our critics there are a dozen who write correctly for every one who writes with individuality, with gusto. But whether it is precision or flavor that is wanting, the cause is the same, and that is a want of regard for the medium of expression. We do not seem to love words as the English and the French love them, and we do not pick them with jealous affection and range them with fastidious care. Wherever we note an exception we should cherish the author as a promise and a possession. It is the rare quality of flavor that makes the value of Mr. Mencken, as it makes the value of Mr. Cabell, not merely in his romances but still more in his books of criticism, in *Straws and Prayer-Books* and *Beyond Life*.

MR. CABELL

One has a way of setting up principles in haste and repenting them at leisure. So it is with my principle—or prejudice—against the use of archaic words. I am strongly of the persuasion that a writer, and especially a writer of prose, should keep to the language of his own time, and that a resort to bookish and archaic diction is a confession of weakness. And so when I began reading Mr. Cabell's *Beyond Life* I said, "This will never do, this affectation of a flavor and a cut of phrase long outmoded. This may be acceptable, and even an added grace, in a *Jurgen* or a *Chivalry*—romances fantastic as a Gothic tapestry; but in a work of sober criticism . . . . !" And I doubted whether I should be able to finish the book. But I got interested in John Charteris and his amusing rehearsal of literary history. Before I knew it he had conducted me from Homer to Marlowe, from Marlowe to Congreve, and from Congreve to Sydnor Harrison. And then, while I still shared the author's notion that this Charteris had been giving us a treatise on the writing of novels, there came his peevish denial of that intention, and I realized that what we had been shown upon this lively screen was a philosophy of life. So that when I turned back to confirm my first impressions on his reprehensible affectation in style, I found that I had above all things a great respect for his spirit and thought.

And long before *Straws and Prayer-Books* came

with its renewed challenge to my pedantry, I realized that I had always been, like everybody else, an affectionate admirer of Charles Lamb, than whom no one ever used more constantly the diction and syntax of old bookish writers. And I remembered that Hazlitt, who wrote incomparably well the plain English of his own day, and on principle preferred the simple and contemporary, had made an exception in the case of Lamb, on the ground that Lamb had so completely assimilated the manner of the seventeenth-century masters that he was practically one of them. And the case of Stevenson next assailed me, a writer whose essays and narratives alike are well spiced with whatever was quaint and racy in the chroniclers of an earlier day. And last I had to acknowledge that I had surrendered completely to the archaism of Charles Doughty, at least in his prose, and—after long challenging his right to the words of Chaucer and Spenser and the King James Bible—had come to the conclusion that nothing could suit better his own spirit and theme in *Arabia Deserta* than this apparel in the antique mode.

In all these cases I concluded it was the fitness of the medium that justified the exception, and its perfect mastery. It suited the man, and moreover he proved his right to it by the fineness of his stroke. Where I object to archaism—and that remains almost everywhere—is in writers of little force and color who try to win from an occasional borrowed word a grace and piquancy that is not in them, pinning on to garments of nondescript plainness some ineffectual patch of scarlet. In the case of Charles Doughty there is the subject: semitic peoples inhabiting a desert bordering on the Holy Land, dwelling in tents, making their stage from well to well like the people of Moses, with, moreover, the lure of buried cities, and ancient inscriptions to be patiently traced by the hand of the archaeologist. But more than that is the man himself, the sincere and cheerful gravity of his approach to life, his rocklike integrity and simplicity of nature, his loyal acceptance of all received values, all manly and humane notions of right and wrong and truth and goodness. All that is biblical and old English. And that is no description at all of John Charteris elaborating his theory of the Demiurge, as he "pretentiously called" the power of romance. Moreover, the locutions of Doughty are biblically plain, compact, and sinewy like monumental inscriptions; they are good as a skilled joiner's work is good; and the smell of them is as the smell of cedarwood, out of the fiber and substance of the thing itself. Whereas the author of *Beyond Life* has described the style of his theorizing novelist in a manner recalling Carlyle's description of the style of Teufelsdröckh, with the same pretense of irritation over his want of naturalness. "Meanwhile he talked: and he talked in very much that redundant and finicky and involved and inverted 'style' of his writings; wherein, as you have probably noted, the infrequent sentence which does not begin with a connective or with an adverb comes as a positive shock. . . . ."

There is in Cabell none of the downrightness of Doughty and the Bible. He writes in the characteristic manner of a scientific age, that hesitating and hairsplitting manner of men seeking the last refinement of truth, full of reservations and qualifications and after-thoughts (the footnotes all included in the text, as De Quincey rather suggests they should be), and with every grade of subordination duly recorded in the flexible medium of adverbial modifiers; that manner with which we have been made so well acquainted by Matthew Arnold and Walter Pater, by Henry James and Marcel Proust. And he has none of the naïveté that gives to Doughty so much of his freshness and sweetness. There is nothing biblical about his thought unless it be the jaded wisdom of Ecclesiastes. He asserts nothing and accepts nothing as truth. All standards and values he brings in question. Men do not appear to him as the central object of God's concern, but as "wingless bipeds . . . . left to their own devices among much non-committal stardrift." Beneath his grinning mask he bears a face both sad and grave, and one comes to understand that he does most decidedly care about man's destiny and the goal of his activities. But he cannot seriously consider that, in the cosmic scale and as judged by reason, any great importance attaches to what man thinks and does. Not wishing to be the fool of his own illusions, he clings instinctively to his tone of playful badinage.

It is clear that Mr. Cabell has not at all the same claim as Mr. Doughty upon the theatrical wardrobe of the old writers. But that he must have some kind of claim upon it is a presumption made stronger by our realization that he is, in general, a master of words, using them with fine and sympathetic discrimination; that he is at infinite pains to seek out the right word; and that he does actually hit upon it much more often than not. He has precision as well as flavor. So that when we find him using tall words, as Hazlitt calls the words of Dr. Johnson, they are not generally "tall, opaque words," as Hazlitt asserts of Dr. Johnson's; some light shines through them of thought and whimsey; and there is a strong presumption that they are not, like the tall words which Mr. Van Vechten transfers so ostentatiously from the dictionary to his romances, a mere pedantic ornament to an otherwise rather undistinguished page. And this is the more likely when we consider that Mr. Cabell has treasured from the old masters not merely the tall words, which were always bookish, but still more the sturdy little words that were never bookish, and are not bookish even now except as, in their modesty and plainness, they have a sharper and brighter appeal to the imagination than their flabby equivalents in contemporary style. Thus in the sentence in which he describes the offering up of the author's life to his art, "He breaks his implements with ruthless usage; he ruins all that time will loan; meanwhile the work *goes forward, with fair promise.*" We have mostly lost the art of saying things with that appealing plainness; we put it in some more roundabout, unimaginative way: "And yet he is making appreciable progress in his work, and has reason for being optimistic." And in our revision we lose both rhythm and savor.

Very often, when we are aware of an antique flavor in Cabell, we can trace it to no form of words not in current usage, but to something more intimate still in his handling of order and syntax, a phrasing no lexicographer would recognize as obsolete, but which does none the less suggest the manner of a seventeenth- or eighteenth-century master by something indefinable—but which at a pinch might be defined!—in the turn of the logic. Speaking of the tendency of an author to use and study his own experience for the benefit of his art, Mr. Cabell says, "All that which is naturally fine in him he will so study, and regard from every aspect, that from much handling it grows dingy." Perfect English of our day, but so fashioned as to suggest the prose of Dryden. He says of Millamant, the famous heroine of Congreve's comedy, "Of course she was the cause that Congreve never married." And we have a thing turned as Bacon might have turned it. Of the effect of Sheridan's speech against Warren Hastings, he says, "I do not expect you to believe this, but it is a matter of record." And we seem to hear the voice of Swift or Arbuthnot. Or he says, "Dryden was a fine poet, and wears Morocco worthily," and we recognize the hand of Lamb.

But now I cannot be persuaded to say that Mr. Cabell is simply an imitator of our fine old writers. I am constrained to hold that, somehow, as with Doughty, though not in the same way as with Doughty, the tinge of archaism suits his turn of thought, serves his purpose, and matches his idiosyncrasy. It suits, for one thing, his type of wit and humor. No, not his type of wit precisely, for in wit there is no type, no new and old. He may suggest the ancients by being witty. But when we actually take under observation an instance of his wit we find nothing archaic in it but the tradition of wit itself. Of clergymen who confuse the material welfare of their own church with the cause of Christianity, he says, "They come to mistake for the light of the world the candle that illuminates the altar." It might have been said by Newman himself. Or again he is discussing the tendency to praise the great classics and leave them unread. "As a case in point, one may well consider that especial glory of English letters, the much-vaunted plays of the Elizabethan and Jacobean dramatists, which justly rank so high in literature that few can endure the altitude." There is here no hint of obsolete or elaborate phrasing. All that Mr. Cabell has done is, with a quick malicious play of wit, to apply literally a figure of speech, taking advantage of one of those analogies in things which it is the nature of the wit and the poet, according to Hobbes, instinctively to perceive.

It must be, strictly speaking, his humor then that suits with the antique and often elaborate fashion of his style. As in Lamb and Carlyle, it is almost invariably a touch of the mock heroic that betrays the mimicry of the old writers. As both Cabell and Carlyle are much beholden to Swift for their manner of expression, so they are both not a little like him in the general view of human kind that makes the substance of their humor. Cabell has none of the savagery of Swift and little of the moral earnestness of Carlyle. In each writer the elements are present in different proportions, but in them all is a strong infusion of both pity and scorn for the race of man, whom they all view from a distant height as if they were gods, albeit with something of the impatience of men judging their fellows. Mr. Cabell's panegyric on Dullness is reminiscent of Swift or Pope. There is something of the *Battle of the Books* in the unctuous learnedness of Charteris and of the editor supplying footnotes to explain the term "prohibitionists," or to explain, of writers like Winston Churchill, to whom Charteris refers, that they were novelists "in vogue at the time he spoke." Some of Mr. Cabell's tall words are typical Carlylese, as where he speaks of "thousands of calligraphic persons," referring to authors who have no more of the divine craft than a fountain pen. Carlyle is a hard hitter; but many of his most telling strokes are made by him when he would stay his hand, and a sudden mildness of understatement betrays a wearied and indulgent judge of human folly! Somewhat in this vein is Mr. Cabell's qualified suggestion that the brain was not originally designed as an implement of authorship. "By any creative writer . . . . the human brain is perverted to uses for which it was perhaps not especially designed; nor is it certain that the human body was originally planned as a device for making marks on paper."

There are several more extensive passages in *Beyond Life* which remind us of Carlyle's ironic view of the vanity of human affairs. There is much of the tone of Teufelsdröckh in the account of how men dress themselves for dances or for church, and go through the motions associated with the idea of amusement or worship—with his wonder at how "the cotillion, or dancing in any form, came to be employed as an arbitrary symbol for amusement." And again there is the passage in the second chapter, reminiscent at once of *Sartor Resartus* and *Pulvis et Umbra*, beginning, "Indeed, when I consider the race to which I have the honor to belong, I am filled with respectful wonder." Cabell is filled with wonder at the obstinacy with which man, in the ignominy and insignificance of his circumstances, yet clings to the idea of his importance. Stevenson is filled with wonder at man's inveterate goodness in these circumstances. Carlyle is filled with wonder at the divinity that gleams out fitfully from the dinginess of his character and surroundings. Carlyle has much more of the Calvinistic earnestness, and constantly sounds the note of evangelical exhortation. The sentence quoted from Cabell has an almost Japanese suavity, he is so politely respectful in his wonder at the race to which he has the honor to belong. His mildness of statement, where he would be ironic, is even milder than Carlyle's and more constant. When Cabell wishes to suggest the extreme indecency of Restoration comedy, and the consequent neglect with which it is treated in our time, he has a way of saying it as different as possible from Macaulay's and easily distinguishable from Lamb's. "But now, in reading, the formal cadences of these elaborate improprieties blend, somehow, into a dirge, hollow and monotonous, over *an era wherein undue importance would seem to have attached to concupiscence.*" Macaulay judges these obsolete plays with the severity of a Puritan magistrate; Lamb praises them with the enthusiasm of an antic humorist. Mr. Cabell accepts them and dismisses them with Congreve's own smile of "amused acquiescence," according to the code of Gallantry which he has erected upon a verse of Horace. He will not take too seriously any of the circus performances of men, having learned to see through all the "illusions" of mankind and judging them in the light of reason, as all of about equally doubtful validity. In such an old gentleman's philosophy there is no call for heavy hitting.

And this reminds us that the flavor of elegant and playful bookishness, with its discreet, pervasive tincture of archaism, is particularly suited to the fundamental attitude of skeptical disillusionment from which Mr. Cabell proceeds. He who questions all values, all those motives of action which Ibsen calls "life lies," and which he more pretentiously denominates "dynamic illusions," naturally shrinks from a blunt and naked blurting out of unamiable doubts. Above all things he wishes to avoid the seriousness of his young contemporaries in American letters. He first invents an aging unsuccessful novelist and eccentric to be the screen between himself and a prying world. And he duly endows him with a style suited to the handling of these touchy matters of belief. For albeit he has been obliged to give up for himself the one great illusion of rationality, he naturally hates like sin to give it up, and still more he hates to have anyone catch him wincing at the odious necessity. And for that matter, he has not altogether given up his illusions; he has merely given up his faith in them as rational. His whole argument is for accepting them, or such of them as most appeal to him; he would have us cling to them as after all "dynamic" and necessary to life.

But still more, in recommending a procedure so irrational, he must avoid anything like a tone of pious gravity; he must involve himself in a cloud of humorous sophistication like an ancient goddess condescending to set foot upon earth. His thesis is very like that of Mr. Santayana in *Poetry and Religion*. Religion Santayana recommends, not because it is true to fact and history, but because it rings true to our hearts, and is current coin in all our transactions with ideal things. But Mr. Cabell is a more nervous and self-conscious thinker. He cannot content himself with the quiet sedateness of a Santayana, philosophically conceding to us all of religion except faith. He cannot himself give up his fundamental illusions without many a grimace of pain; and his notions of gallantry prescribe that his grimaces shall be comic ones. He wants us to understand that, while he has made a formal sacrifice of his reason, it is lively enough for all that, and will have its revenge wherever it can upon the imperious instincts that have repudiated it. Romance, which is a kind of faith, he has finally espoused. But like so many other true believers, he has come to his faith by way of the dark wood of utter skepticism. And he is forever casting nervous glances over his shoulder, in the manner of Lot's wife, at the darkness whence he has so recently emerged. So that his most eloquent passages, such as those in which Charteris sums up the qualities which he craves in literature and life, are shot through with whimsical concessions to the vigilant and fleering spirit of irony.

So I in point of fact desire of literature, just as you guessed, precisely those things of which I most poignantly and most constantly feel the lack in my own life. And it is that which romance affords her postulants. The philtres of romance are brewed to free us from this unsatisfying life that is calendered by fiscal years, and to contrive a less disastrous elusion of our own personalities than many seek dispersedly in drink and drugs and lust and fanaticism, and sometimes in death. For, beset by his own rationality, the normal man is goaded to evade the strictures of his normal life, upon the incontestable ground that it is a stupid and unlovely routine; and to escape likewise from his own personality, which bores him quite as much as it does his associates. So he hurtles into these very various roads from reality, precisely as a goaded sheep flees without notice of what lies ahead. . . . . .

And romance tricks him, but not to his harm. For, be it remembered that man alone of animals plays the ape to his dreams. Romance it is undoubtedly who whispers to every man that life is not a blind and aimless business, not all a hopeless waste and confusion; and that his existence is a pageant (appreciatively observed by divine spectators), and that he is strong and excellent and wise: and to romance he listens, willing and thrice willing to be cheated by the honeyed fiction. The things of which romance assures him are very far from true:

yet it is solely by believing himself a creature but little lower than the cherubim that man has by interminable small degrees become, upon the whole, distinctly superior to the chimpanzee: so that, however extravagant may seem these whispers today, they were immeasurably more remote from veracity when men first began to listen to their sugared susurrus, and steadily the discrepancy lessens. Today these things seem quite as preposterous to calm consideration as did flying yesterday: and so, to the Gradgrindians, romance appears to discourse foolishly, and incurs the common fate of prophets: for it is about tomorrow and about the day after tomorrow, that romance is talking, by means of parables. And all the while man plays the ape to fairer and yet fairer dreams, and practise strengthens him at mimickry. . . . .

To what does the whole business tend?—why, how in heaven's name should I know? We can but be content to note that all goes forward, toward something. . . . . It may be that we are nocturnal creatures perturbed by rumors of a dawn which comes inevitably, as prologue to a day wherein we and our children have no part whatever. It may be that when our arboreal propositus descended from his palm-tree and began to walk upright about the earth, his progeny were forthwith committed to a journey in which today is only a way-station. Yet I prefer to take it that we are components of an unfinished world, and that we are but as seething atoms which ferment toward its making, if merely because man as he now exists can hardly be the finished product of any Creator whom one could very heartily revere. We are being made into something quite unpredictable, I imagine: and through the purging and the smelting, we are sustained by an instinctive knowledge that we are being made into something better. For this we know, quite incommunicably, and yet as surely as we know that we will have it thus.

And it is this will that stirs in us to have the creatures of earth and the affairs of earth, not as they are, but "as they ought to be," which we call romance. But when we note how visibly it sways all life we perceive that we are talking about God.

And so I have been at great pains to explain and justify a lively manner of writing which needs no more explaining than the simple statement that the author has a lively mind and takes pleasure in giving it exercise. For Mr. Cabell may have lost all his illusions; but he has clearly not lost, what is better than any illusion, the pleasure he takes in setting words in order. He may dismiss as a romantic illusion the author's earnestness in seeking the approval of posterity; but the gusto he betrays in every turn of his thought shows there is present a joyous and instinctive play of the mind which has no need of an illusion to motive it, however much it may call for one to "rationalize" it. These "dynamic" illusions, this realism and romance, and doubt and faith, are but as balls which the juggler shies into the air, three or four at a time, by way of showing how many he can keep going at once. The argument of the book is as a tight rope on which he can balance himself, with an ease, the gift of natural grace and long practice, which disguises the extreme difficulty of the trick. He is at one with all lovers of paradox, the Chestertons and Shaws, the Swifts and Frances—those subtle and lively thinkers in whom one thought begets another, assertion begets denial, denial assertion, and ideas come to stand upon their feet only when they are tired of standing on their heads. There is in him that mocking, will-o'-the-wisp spirit, "now you have me and now you don't," which is the delight of jesting Pilates, and a thorn in the flesh of those who are forever staying for an answer.

In short, he has drunken of the Holy Bottle—for I will make my own interpretation of Rabelais' oracle; and so inspired, he cannot content himself with those sober words and turns of thought which serve the purpose of more placid men. There are other ways of manifesting literary gusto, but this is Cabell's way. And gusto is, according to his Charteris, a quality always distinguishable in books that are to endure.

They have a heartiness akin to the smacking of lips over a good dish. . . . . It is not ecstasy, although to ecstasy it may approach. I think it is almost a physical thing: it certainly involves a complete surrender to life, and an absorption of one's self in the functions of being. It is a drunkenness of the soul, perhaps; it is allied to that fierce pain and joy which we call ecstatic living, and which the creative artist must always seek to reproduce in his work. . . . .

THE HOLY BOTTLE

MR. MENCKEN

It is this gusto which gives to Cabell his distinction among American writers of prose and leads one to dwell upon him with satisfaction; and it is likewise gusto which gives one satisfaction in the writing of Mr. Mencken. There are many ways of manifesting gusto, and the way of Mr. Mencken is in some directions as different as possible from that of Mr. Cabell. His writing is not involved and inverted; it is redundant in a very different manner from that of Mr. Cabell; and it is finicky in no manner whatsoever. He is too downright for any connectives but adversatives, and too positive for any adverbial modifiers save those that make for superlative emphasis. His great delight is to "have at" his subject, or his victim; hammer and tongs are his favorite weapons; and he has no patience with the elaborate ceremonial of a courtly fencing-match *à la* Tybalt.

Mr. Mencken has a great fondness for certain unusual words, some of them a bit archaic in flavor, but they are seldom of the elegant, bookish sort fancied by Mr. Cabell. They fall into several simple categories. There are words of a scientific provenance, used almost invariably with a drollery and appropriateness that is their justification and entirely clears the author of a suspicion of naïve pedantry. If he uses "agronomist" for farmer and "staphylococci" for the familiar lice, it is in his apt rendering of the politician's idealized figure of the husbandman, and it is but a burlesque extension of the politician's own euphuistic style. We have of course his predilection for putting men into generic classes with labels, *homo americanus*, etc., for the joy of seeing them wriggle. He has retained from his legal studies a few simple terms, English and Latin, to give a burlesque tincture of learning and authority to his ex cathedra pronouncements. And he keeps in use a select list of anatomical terms; therewith he may give a Rabelaisian heartiness, for example, to his account of the passion of certain of our critics for "flogging the corpse of poor Jean-Jacques."

Do the *Chandala* rise from their sewers and rat-holes, and demand places at the table where the pie is? Then into the fire with his tibia, his fibula, his radius, his ulna, his os ilium, his sternum! Is democracy a murrain upon all of us? Then let the faithful house-dog (*Canis*) gnaw the rest of his bones!

And that is about all that can be cited against him in the way of tall words. I will not say that Mr. Mencken has not a love of curious, outlandish words. But I say, in the first place, that that is a most healthy passion provided it be kept in hand. In the second place, I say that he does make them serve his purpose most fitly. And, finally, I remark that what he keeps alive of old English words are not those lace bordered and smelling of musk, but mainly those sharp and serviceable little words which have largely gone out of polite usage, but which he is fortunately not too fine to have taken to his bosom, and which are like the proverbial peasant blood so much desiderated for the renewal of princely stocks. He tells us of the gaudy yarns of modern vice-crusaders and of the bounce and gusto that attached in the Middle Ages to the game of putting down crime. His mainstay is that class of opprobrious epithets in which the English and every vigorous language is rich, which lend themselves to the inspiriting art of calling names. Cheats and fools are for him, as they were for the Elizabethans, a fruitful source of inspiration, and he loves to sing of coney-catchers, bawds, and pimps; of cheapjacks and zanies and yokels; of scoundrels and rascals and poltroons. He goes to the Orient for mullahs and fellahin and voodooism and jehads, all terms to characterize opprobriously the cultural levels of the "hinterland." He loves those geographic designations that so effectually put in their place Kansas and Arkansas—the Christian Endeavor belt and the foreign-missions belt; and he is never tired of inventing terms for getting under the skin of the alfalfa colleges and the rustic Ph.D.'s.

There is more here than malice and meanness, smartness and odium theologicum, which, we must all agree, are spiritual vices. There are rare literary virtues involved, such as imagination and enterprise, and that zest for words which is one-half of the motive of Renaissance philosophers for indulging that same theological malice. Mr. Mencken has Rabelais' own love for piling up vigorous little words from the vernacular, words of racy savor and corporal reference, and putting them alongside of learned words in an argument conducted with all the punctilio of formal logic. For the life of Panurge was as close to the soil as his speculations were soaring and airy. In this spirit is that essay in the fourth series of *Prejudices* entitled "Essay in Constructive Criticism," in which he pretends to offer his own system of government, and especially the pages in which, in somewhat the grave, argumentative manner of Swift, he proposes a new way of dealing with corrupt officials. This essay was inspired by the great exposure of public corruption in and following the term of office of Mr. Daugherty, and the picture the author sketches of aggrieved individuals dealing corporally with the offending magistrate may serve as a kind of catharsis to purge the soul of the reader and bring him back to a normal faith in human justice.

THE HOLY BOTTLE

To punish a judge taken in judicial crim.con. by fining him or sending him to jail is a bit too facile and obvious. What is needed is a system (*a*) that does not depend for its execution upon the good-will of job-holders, and (*b*) that provides swift, certain and unpedantic punishments, each fitted neatly to its crime. Such a system, after due prayer, I have devised. It is simple, it is unhackneyed, and I believe that it would work. It is divided into two halves. The first half takes the detection and punishment of the crimes of job-holders away from courts of impeachment, congressional smelling committees, and other such agencies—*i.e.*, away from other job-holders—and vests it in the whole body of free citizens, male and female. The second half provides that any member of that body, having looked into the acts of a job-holder and found him delinquent, may punish him instantly and on the spot, and in any manner that seems appropriate and convenient—and that in case this punishment involves physical damage to the job-holder, the ensuing inquiry by the grand jury or coroner shall confine itself strictly to the question whether the job-holder deserved what he got. In other words, I propose it shall be no longer *malum in se* for a citizen to pummel, cow-hide, kick, gouge, cut, wound, bruise, maim, burn, club, bastinado, flay or even lynch a job-holder, and that it shall be *malum prohibitum* only to the extent that the punishment exceeds the job-holder's deserts. The amount of this excess, if any, may be determined very conveniently by a petit jury, as other questions of guilt are now determined. The flogged judge, or Congressman, or Prohibition officer, or any other job-holder, on being discharged from hospital—or his chief heir, in case he has perished—goes before a grand jury and makes complaint, and, if a true bill is found, a petit jury is empanelled and all the evidence is put before it. If it decides that the job-holder deserved the punishment inflicted upon him, the citizen who inflicted it is acquitted with honor. If, on the contrary, it decides that this punishment was excessive, then the citizen is adjudged guilty of assault, mayhem, murder, or whatever it is, in a degree apportioned to the difference between what the job-holder deserved and what he got, and punishment for that excess follows in the usual course.

The beauty of this is not that it is a *reductio ad absurdum* of democratic administration—if that is what it is; for I confess I have never been able to get a clear idea of Mr. Mencken's political system. The beauty is that it gives a lively picture of the citizen executing ideal justice, and puts the right feeling into the reader's nerves and muscles. The touch about the hospital is most fetching, and the list of verbs to designate the punishment has all the "bounce and gusto" of Panurge sending overboard Dingdong with his sheep or rolling the dung-cart down hill on the watchmen of Paris. They have that direct physical appeal that makes the strength of Swift's theological fable in *A Tale of a Tub*. One of the great virtues of Mr. Mencken's style is that he has command of those verbs which show as well as say, for which Stevenson is so highly regarded. The judges do not lay aside their judicial functions; they "climb down from their benches and clamor obscenely for votes."

For Mencken, too, has drunken of the Holy Bottle, and while we may not be able, in this or that matter, to take his doctrine seriously or even to make out just what it is, we cannot but be infected with his joy in the work of setting words in order. He himself affirms, in his "Footnote on Criticism," that he has no messianic motive in writing. His motive is "no more and no less than the simple desire to function freely and beautifully, to give outward and objective form to ideas that bubble inwardly and have a fascinating lure to them, to get rid of them dramatically and make an articulate noise in the world." He always carries a high head of steam, which shows itself among other things in the great positiveness of all his statements. The more questionable a proposition may be, the more certain it is to be for Mr. Mencken "obvious to an impartial observer." Where the grounds of some matter are complicated he finds without fail "the plain and simple reason." The aim of the injunction clause in the Volstead Act is "simply and solely" such and such. As for Emerson, "The *whole* system of his ideas was an *unqualified* protest against hampering traditions of *every* sort," and "If he were alive today he would not be with the professors but *unalterably* against them."

And this is for the most part sufficiently exhilarating. This is, literally, bounce and gusto. Cabell has taken from Carlyle his manner of understatement and soft-voiced humorous insinuation; Mencken has taken his overstatement and burly "frightfulness." If perhaps Mr. Cabell's system is more certain to endear him to a critical posterity, Mr. Mencken's has won him a wide and respectful hearing among contemporaries who are fonder of the brasses than the wood winds. And the respectful interest of contemporaries is no small recommendation to posterity. The figure of the brasses I borrow from Mr. Mencken himself, who says that his "murmur [against the farmers] is scored in the manner of Berlioz, for ten thousand trombones *fortissimo*."

Mr. Cabell's style is that of old Charteris setting forth his views to a sympathetic disciple in the seclusion of a midnight library. Mr. Mencken's is that of midday and the market place. His liveliness and crispness and pungency are forensic virtues, as his sentence-structure and rhythm are forensic. He has always in mind an audience that cannot take in long sentences or a manner of statement devious or involved. He has always in mind an adversary who must be answered or an opposed opinion which must be demolished to the satisfaction of all present. His sentences individually and his sentence-groups tend to the antithetic and to forms calculated for the presentation of sharp contrasts. His introductory clauses tend to be concessive statements or such as present a partial or specious aspect of the matter, leading to the opposed affirmation of absolute and final truth. He has not infrequently several statements in sequence in which, in identical form, he marshals the separate items of his indictment. He is, with due allowances made, the Macaulay to Cabell's Pater. He speaks of the federal judge under the Volstead Act:

Once the dispenser of varieties of law that only scoundrels questioned, he is now the harassed and ludicrous dispenser of varieties of law that only idiots approve. . . . . Once the equal of an archbishop, he is now the equal of a police captain; once respected, he is now distrusted and disliked. . . . .

It is their theory, apparently, that the sole function of a judge is to fill the jails. If the accused happens to be guilty or to be reasonably suspected of guilt, well and good. But if, as in the Chicago Socialist trials, he is obviously innocent, to hell with him anyhow. True enough, a majority of the Federal judges, high and low, still stand clear of such buffooneries. Even in the midst of the worst hysteria of the war there were plenty who refused to be run amok by Palmer, Burleson and company; I need cite only Hand, J., and Rose, J., as admirable examples of a number of judges who preserved their dignity 'mid the rockets' red glare. But the headlines in the newspapers had nothing to say about such judges. Etc.

. . . . [The prevailing view] is a view which, in brief, holds that the Federal bench is no longer the most exalted and faithful protector of the liberties of the citizen, but the most relentless and inordinate foe of them—that its main purpose is not to dispense justice at all, but to get men into jail, guilty or not guilty, by fair means or foul—that to this end it is willing to lend itself to the execution of any law, however extravagant, and to support that execution with a casuistry that is flatly against every ordinary conception of common sense and common decency.

Here is a form all straight lines and sharp angles, where Mr. Cabell's is all curves and spirals. It is even better adapted to the more obvious types of paradox and epigram. Mr. Mencken can say, of a man's treatment of his wife, "He can never, of course, deceive her utterly, but if he is skillful he may at least deceive her enough to make her happy." For Mr. Mencken is clearly one of those who walk tight ropes and shy up balls and keep them going. He is one of the band whose delight is in the free play of the mind, and has his place with the Swifts and Shaws, the Frances and Voltaires. He is indeed more classical, or "dry," in his style than Mr. Cabell, whose manner has in it an element not present in that of Swift and Shaw, of Schopenhauer and Voltaire: an element that informs the rhythm and movement and gives it an effect very different from that of those who work without mortar and lay squared block to squared block. Cabell is in the tradition of De Quincey and the more romantic stylists, who are concerned—sometimes to their own undoing—with the large and pulsing flow of the discourse. There is here no tap-tap of the hammer, no sense of sharp transitions, but the passage from phrase to phrase is like the smooth break of wave overlapping wave. The guiding instinct is for symmetry; and while there is a plentiful use of antithesis, the antithesis is sought for the sake of balance, and not the balance for the sake of antithesis. There is that love of words and phrases going in pairs, of the thing said twice, which is so notable in the prose of Milton, of Addison, of Ruskin. And one pair springs from another like the new pink leaves of the wintergreen from the stalk that bears the leaves of last year and the year before. The author loves to pile up item upon item, but assiduously he avoids monotony and obviousness by an infinite slight variation in the turn of the phrase. He loves, like De Quincey and Pater, a period built up and sustained by a series of little touches, easily and without the strain of German periods upon the memory, and falling gently at the end in a studied cadence. His *sostenuto* is like that of a bird sailing long and far, with an occasional slight movement of the wings to keep it going.

This is the dithyrambic style, and has in it the lift and excitement of song. It seems to be written to music and to be accompanied by hidden strings. But there is likewise in the nervous prose of Mencken the excitement of an accelerated heartbeat. His staccato and Cabell's legato are two kindred ways of expressing the same artistic impulse. The violinist takes equal delight in the smooth, sustained note and the group of notes clipped and crisp as a shower of spray. Neither of these men deigns for long to set foot on the ground, for they have both drunken of the Holy Bottle.

MR. SHERMAN

When I look about for a third writer of serious prose to set with these as evidence of promise for an American art, the one who first suggests himself is Mr. Sherman. He is perhaps, with Mr. Mencken, our most prominent critic; he has important things to say, and he says them with a competence that is not to be questioned. Moreover, for one, like me, who is engaged in the teaching of the young, he cannot but appeal by virtue of his judicial and open-minded approach to the moot questions of present-day life, and particularly the question of what is to be recommended to the young in the way of reading matter.

There is one very great writer with whom Mr. Sherman almost infallibly suggests comparison. For he is concerned with our national ideals much as Matthew Arnold was concerned with the national ideals of the English. He has something of the same judicial and broad-minded spirit. He keeps his temper. He does not jump to conclusions, but likes to draw distinctions, to make definitions, and to trace things back to first principles. He does not trust to legislative enactments and government censorships so much as to the force of enlightened opinion. His discussion of the censorship of "obscene" books is conducted in much the temper in which Arnold might have conducted it, and his conclusion is such as Arnold might have reached. He opposes the censorship of serious works of literature, but he distinguishes among the many conflicting reasons urged for such opposition, and he does not propose to leave the situation to take care of itself. He is not unduly gloomy over the present state of religion and culture. Like Arnold, he is willing to pronounce a coroner's verdict of death upon beliefs that are actually dead, and to find the hope of the future in tendencies present in our life though not yet prevailing.

The resemblance is still more striking when it comes to his tactics and rhetorical procedure. His "dear Cornelia" serves the purpose of Herr von Thunder-ten-Tronckh in *Friendship's Garland* and of Mr. Roebuck and other persons quoted in *Culture and Anarchy*. Such figures give a touch of fictional liveliness to an abstract theme, and call out the conversational manner which the author loves, giving play to his humor and urbanity. It is, however, in his essay entitled "Towards an American Type" that his dialectics are most closely modeled upon Arnold's. He has the same easy way of representing himself as a sort of modern Socrates going about asking people serious questions. The three men with whom he had recently talked so long serve as Arnoldian provocation to his discourse. "There were brains and money and power behind them; and they were hunting for adequate objects on which to expend them." The university colleague who questions Mr. Sherman's optimism over the state of the university community is the challenger who plays so large a part in Arnold; and Mr. Sherman's humility in regard to his origins is like Arnold's acknowledgment that he is himself a member of the Philistine middle class, and that, as Frederic Harrison has pointed out, he is without the discipline of philosophy. "My friend knows that I belong to the western rabble by birth and residence; and he has lived so long among us that he has acquired our western habit of calling a spade a spade." Again, Mr. Sherman's selection of the phrase, "athletic asceticism"—"I choose the word 'asceticism' because it will be noticed and challenged, under the impression that asceticism means something sour, crabbed, thin, and starved"—and his way of defining this word, as well as elsewhere the word "Puritan," by discriminating its current meaning from that which it should bear, remind one of Arnold's famous definition of "culture."

But most like Arnold is Mr. Sherman's manner of marshaling his heads of discourse (the things in which Americans all effectively believe), and the pertinacity with which he repeats in each case the neat little formula that applies, making clear the significance of each point in the general argument.

It signifies [the prevalence of plumbing] that every civilized man, woman and child in the United States *believes in* being clean, *and in what is compatible with that, and disbelieves* in being dirty, and in what conduces to being dirty. It is a little point, but it is something that we agree on. *The whole pressure of the American community is towards being* physically clean. . . . . Well, there is something definite that we *all believe in;* and are thankful for.

I turned in another direction. . . . . I asked what the benevolent millionaires were expending their millions for; I found that they were pouring their millions into research for the extinction of pestilence, for the wiping out of hookworm, and yellow fever, and tuberculosis, and cancer, and all forms of communicable disease. And it appeared to me obvious that *the American people believe in* health and youth, and are anxious and happy to invest heavily in them; and that *they disbelieve in whatever is incompatible with* health and the preservation of youth. There is another definite point for belief and religious gratitude.

. . . . It means [the large expenditure for schools] that *the American people believe in* becoming intelligent just as fast as they can, *and that they disbelieve in whatever is incompatible with that.* . . . .

I turned in another direction. . . . . [The business men] *believe in* publicity. . . . . [The business man] wishes as a business man and a producer to be able to stand the critical scrutiny of a hundred million pairs of eyes. He *believes in everything that is* compatible with that, and eventually he is going to *believe in nothing that is incompatible with that*. The *pressure* of a hundred million pairs of critical eyes is a tremendous molding *pressure*. *The entire pressure* of the American community is *towards* preparing a man *to stand inspection*, and *whatever is compatible with that*. Somehow, we may say, the man who is ready *to stand inspection* mostly seems to take hold of circumstances at the right end. The ethical implications of being able *to stand inspection* are immense.

. . . . Then I said to myself, *the people of the United States believe in* automobiles *and what is compatible with them, and they disbelieve in what is incompatible with* automobiles. They believe in, they rejoice in, swift mobility. They believe in being private engineers. Their delight is in driving a forty- or seventy-horse-power machine from place to place at a speed of from twenty to sixty miles an hour; and *they believe in whatever is compatible with that*. The ethical implications of being a private engineer are immense; but we have hardly begun to recognize what they are.

Now I have always admired Arnold's deliberate and pertinacious way of repeating his key-phrases at intervals throughout his discussion, especially in *Culture and Anarchy*, and I cannot agree with Mr. Saintsbury that he wrote better before he took on this mannerism. It is not indeed a practice to be recommended to others, and it is hard to say just what there is in Arnold's handling of the device that gives

its particular quality in him, its more than rhetorical effectiveness, even its subtlety of effect. There
is, for one thing, the manner in which the repeated
words are brought in, the suppleness of thought of
the sentences in which they are imbedded, the modification of light thrown upon them by varied angles
of approach. There is also the ingenious combination of several sets of key-phrases, bearing various
relations to one another, in an intricate and changing pattern of thought. In his famous lecture on
"Literature and Science" Arnold brings in at least
a dozen times his motive of "the sense we have in
us for conduct, the sense we have in us for beauty."
But he has a half-dozen slight variations upon this
phrasing: the power of conduct, the power of
beauty; the desire; and the instinct; and the need;
and the necessity. Moreover, this theme receives its
development along with and through the impulse of
other themes, which color it with tinctures of wit
and eloquence, so that when one arrives at his final
gravely cadenced prediction that "the majority of
men will always require humane letters; and so
much the more, as they have the more and the greater results of science to relate to the need in man for
conduct, and to the need in him for beauty," one
has not the sense of a phrase worn threadbare with
overmuch use, but rather the sense of an idea, or a

musical theme, ingeniously developed to the full satisfaction of the mind.

And then there is the delicate spice of whimsical wit that pervades so much of Arnold's best writing, and that is one manifestation in him of a rich though quiet gusto. There is a subtle, ironic manipulation of the thought so as to set a trap for the unwary victim. The repeated phrase is like a move in chess, each move bringing the adversary a little nearer to a checkmate. Most amusing in this kind is his little game with Mr. Roebuck and his oft-reiterated boast that every man in England may say what he likes, where Arnold counters with the assertion that "the aspirations of culture . . . . are not satisfied unless what men say, when they may say what they like, is worth saying. . . . ." But more elaborate, and more remarkable for its interwoven themes, is his grave little wrestling bout with English Puritanism going under the innocuous denomination of "the passion for doing good."

Only, whereas the passion for doing good is apt to be over-hasty in determining what reason and the will of God say, because its turn is for acting rather than thinking and it wants to be beginning to act; and whereas it is apt to take its own conceptions, which proceed from its own state of development and share in all the imperfections and immaturities of this, for a basis of action; what distinguishes culture is, that it is possessed by the scientific passion as well as by the passion of doing good; that it demands worthy notions of reason and the will of God, and does not readily suffer its own crude conceptions to substitute themselves for them. And knowing that no action or institution can be salutary and stable which is not based on reason and the will of God, it is not so bent on acting and instituting, even with the great aim of diminishing human error and misery ever before its thoughts, but that it can remember that acting and instituting are of little use, unless we know how and what we ought to act and to institute.

As for Mr. Sherman's use of Arnoldian repetition, I do not think so good a case can be made out for it. It does serve for clearness and to clench his argument, and satisfies the more obvious requirements of good writing. But it does not give one, to the same degree, the impression of subtlety and elegance. Mr. Sherman's sentences are certainly wrought with competence. He says what he wants to say with lucidity and force. Broadly speaking, his rhythms are of the same general pattern as Mr. Mencken's. They are straightforward and right angled; they are crisp and downright. It is in general good, strong, serviceable writing. But it is clearly not the writing of a Matthew Arnold. In recommending to the American people to cultivate that "athletic asceticism" in which they already believe Mr. Sherman was undertaking a much less exacting task than Arnold in recommending to the English people a culture which was so much in need of expounding and making palatable; and he has no need of the refinements of thought which give to the sentences and rhythms of Arnold so much of their subtle charm and beauty.

In fact, Mr. Sherman does not give one the impression of caring much for beauty. He has the air of a man of affairs with a strong sense of his obligations to society. But of emotion he seems to have little, and in the last analysis it is his lack of emotion that keeps him from having the appeal of an Arnold. There is nothing which he seems to love as Arnold loved that "adorable dreamer," his alma mater. I feel in him no such lift of the imagination as where Arnold speaks of his own time as one of those "times of faith and ardour, times when the intellectual horizon is opening and widening all around us."

It is natural that Mr. Sherman should not make a great show of emotion when you consider the objectives which he proposes for us. They are wholesome, practical objectives, such as a sensible man would set for himself as at least incidental to the main purpose of living. But they are not the main purpose of living as proposed by an Arnold or a Cabell. Mr. Sherman finds that the American people have a natural liking to be clean, to be healthful, to be intelligent, to be able to stand the inspection of their hundred million compatriots, to drive fast machines, and to engage in athletic games; and he recommends that they cultivate themselves along these lines, and rule out of their lives everything, like strong drink, that is incompatible with these pursuits. Of his six objectives only one has anything to do with the pursuits of the mind; and that aim of being intelligent he dismisses with a word as if it were of secondary importance. This is all very different from Matthew Arnold's recommendation, along with the passion for doing good, of the passion for beauty and the scientific passion (that is, a "desire after the things of the mind simply for their own sakes and for the pleasure of seeing them as they are") as the primary aims of life. It is very different from the pleasure dwelt on by Mr. Cabell, which "one man derives from writing the Second Part of *Faust*, and another from playing chess,—the pleasure of using the finest part of your mind, such as it is, to its fullest extent."

I feel quite sure that Mr. Sherman is not writing with his tongue in his cheek; the essay in question bears all the marks of being a serious exhortation addressed primarily to university students. It is wholesome advice to university students, as far as it goes, but it is not inspiring advice to them or to anyone else. I believe that Mr. Sherman has underrated the disinterestedness of at least the best part of our university students. They care more about being inspired than about being guided safely, or flattered in their own predilections; and they will follow the inspiring preacher who sends them to be missionaries in Africa or who sets up some vision of "sweetness and light." If they have read the classics, they know that Athens has something more to offer than the "athletic asceticism" perpetuated in marble, as Mr. Sherman points out, by the Greek sculptors; there was the art of the sculptors themselves and of the poets, the cult of beauty; there was the study of perfection, intellectual and moral; and there was the scientific passion for seeing things as in themselves they really are.

Mr. Sherman was not writing with his tongue in his cheek, but he was in a manner writing down to his university students and other athletic Americans. The objectives which he recommends for his typical American are of course not those toward which he himself labors in his scholarly studies, in his art of criticism, in his ceaseless effort to shape and refine his philosophy of life. He is indulging himself in the pleasure of using the finest part of his mind, which is not at all a practical business; and that is why, in his recommendations to his readers to indulge their bent for athletic asceticism, we are

aware of a half-hearted tone, a note of disingenuousness. I do not mean to imply that he is conscious-
ly disingenuous. But he has allowed himself to be
molded by the views of a sensible and practical
world, and he no doubt believes that it is first of all
necessary to recommend a sensible and practical line
of action. He believes that degeneracy is the chief
menace of any civilization and that eternal vigilance
is demanded of us if we are to make ourselves safe
against degeneracy. And his energies are so absorbed
in the strain of vigilance that he has little left for
beauty and verve and the useless and unpractical
flowers of art. His case is not, indeed, so extreme
as that of other critics, like Mr. Babbitt or Mr.
More, whose ruling motive is anxiety over the
spiritual predicament of our race, and to whom one
can only repeat the words of Tranio in *The Taming
of the Shrew:*

> Let's be no stoicks nor no stocks, I pray,
> Or so devote to Aristotle's checks
> As Ovid be an outcast quite abjured.
> . . . .
> No profit grows where is no pleasure ta'en.

Mr. Sherman has not lost his humor and his wit.
He has not lost touch with common life and the man
in the street. But he is still a bit too sensible and
too responsible. He will not let himself go. He has

missed that gusto which approaches to ecstasy, which "involves a complete surrender to life, and an absorption of one's self in the functions of being."

He has missed an artistic distinction which much less responsible writers do not lack. On the surface he may seem a fairer critic than Mr. Mencken, and more serious. But it is so often a seriousness within limits—within the limits of a sensible Weltanschauung. Mr. Mencken may be as reckless as you please. He may even be prone to force his voice beyond its natural pitch of scorn and ridicule, to furnish copy for the press. But we remember that even Carlyle was unable to stop the flow of his railing, and that he often, as the years went on, seemed a parody of himself. And I have not felt that, on the whole, Mr. Mencken has ceased to take pleasure in his writing, or that his railing has ceased to have in it a core of honest feeling. There is very little in him of the constructive critic. One can with difficulty learn what it is he would approve in literary art, or the art of living, and the only things he seems to admire are the novels of Dreiser and the symphonies of Beethoven. But there is one fair word that occasionally makes itself heard in the midst of his storming, the word "honor," so much fairer and more inspiring than "athleticism" or "asceticism." And there are all those salt and saucy words that never fail to season his most incidental utterance. His rhythms are, as I have said, broadly speaking, of the same general pattern as Mr. Sherman's. But there is more go to them, more nervous vigor. His sentences ring with a clink of steel, and that is a kind of music. He does not seem to be deliberately cultivating beauty like Mr. Cabell. But beauty is a word of wider extension in our day than in the time of Tennyson and Chopin; and, with the sound in our ears of Strawinsky, of Honegger and Bela Bartok, we hesitate to deny beauty to the prose of Mencken. Anything so lean and pointed as this, anything so joyously athletic, must have its beauty. We have so little prose of salt and savor that we cannot afford to be sniffy with Mr. Mencken. His sentences have not that silver ring of Mr. Cabell's, nor do we seem to hear them flowing on to the sound of hidden strings. But the ring of steel is music, too. Perhaps he fences in time, to the sound of fifes and drums. He has the distinction of those who are not afraid to make a complete surrender to life, who have drunk without question of the Holy Bottle.

AUGUST, 1925

PROUD WORDS

PROUD WORDS

Look out how you use proud words.
When you let proud words go, it is
not easy to call them back.
—CARL SANDBURG

THE author of *This Freedom*, in telling us of the great moderation of his hero in the use of swear-words, refers to our age as one "given to easy freedom of language." This is not the freedom to which he refers in the title. It may be that he was obscurely conscious of a certain easy freedom of his own in the use of our mother-tongue. And this reminds one of what, in last year's book,[1] the same author has to say about the favorite words of his heroine and her husband: "Why, Tony and I get fond of a word and then we have it for our own, whichever of us it is, and use it for everything." One at once thinks of Mr. Hutchinson himself and of many others of the writing craft.

Professor Kittredge used to point out how this was characteristic of no less a writer than Shake-

[1] Note the date of writing given at the end of the essay.

speare—how Shakespeare in a certain year would be obsessed with a word or figure and return to it as much as twice within the same play! In the current novelists this kind of obsession is more obstinate. It sometimes lasts through a considerable period of years: the favorite word appears in book after book, and sometimes as often as dozens or scores of times within a book; and it is much more suggestive of an easy freedom of language than anything in Shakespeare.

But what must be most discouraging to the authors themselves is that fine words are catching, and no writer, however curious he may be in searching them out for himself, can ever for a long while "have them for his own." One of the words of the year in 1922 was undoubtedly the vigorous adjective "devastating." Who invented it, I do not know, but it has clearly come into vogue. The publishers of Mr. Hecht's *Gargoyles* let us know on the cover that it is a devastating book. The publishers of Mr. Swinnerton's *The Three Lovers* let us know that, in this latest of his productions, he has given us unusually prolonged and devastating revelations of the hearts and brains of girls. In this case the publishers have but taken the cue from the author himself, for more than once he makes effective use of the forceful new word.

Mr. Walpole uses the word in more than one place in *The Cathedral*, and with evident pride and deliberation. Amy Brandon is represented as being devoured by "the one dominating, devastating desire she had ever known." (One might assume that one such desire would be all one could know in a lifetime.) And Falk Brandon had a secret preoccupation that seemed "so absorbing and devastating to him that he could not believe that every one around him would not guess it. . . . . His secret was quite simply that, for the last year, he had been devastated by the consciousness of Annie Hogg, the daughter of the landlord of The Dog and Pilchard! Yes, devastated was the word."

There seems to be a slight anachronism here; it does not seem possible that, away back in the eighteen-nineties, the archdeacon's son could have been so sure that that was the word. But it is clear enough that, a generation later, it perfectly satisfies the taste of Mr. Walpole. And in *This Freedom* Mr. Hutchinson makes his usual improvements on other people's words by speaking of an act of Rosalie's father which "proved to be but a stagger down into morass heavier and more *devastating of ambition*."

The word "devastating" makes its appeal on two distinct grounds. It is violent, superlative; and it is, or was a year ago, unusual in its application. It was thought to be *recherché;* the discerning reader is likely to call it affected. And it is the affectation with which we are concerned in the present essay.

One of our most enterprising writers is Mr. Hergesheimer; and he is given to renewing his stock of expressive words more often than most. It is particularly edifying to note in his case the change of fashion from year to year. Often the favored word is used correctly; often it is used with an easy freedom, in some sense of his own, not yet recorded in the dictionaries. In 1917, in *The Three Black Pennys*, the word of the year was "paramount." And so fond was Mr. Hergesheimer of this word, so persuaded was he that he "had it for his own," that he was inclined to "use it for everything," at least for everything remarkable or extreme—and things remarkable or extreme were very common in *The Three Black Pennys*. "Her discontent was paramount. It was deeper than he had supposed. . . . . A paramount situation to which he lacked the key. . . . . A small reason for withholding any paramount salvation. . . . . Caught in the flood of her paramount disdain."

Year before last, in *Cytherea*, the favorite word was the adjective "engaging," together with the related noun and verb. Everything that was attractive to Lee Randon is represented as engaging—dresses, people, and even the room in the Inglaterra Hotel. That is a good word and, used with proper regard to English usage, Mr. Hergesheimer might have found it in Henry James. The freedom lies only in the frequency of its use, the strain put upon it. But Mr. Hergesheimer is not content with the adjective. He is so "intrigued"—if I may use a word of kindred spirit, a favorite of Mr. Swinnerton's—he is so intrigued with the adjective that he must draw in the verb and noun. Our Yankee writer becomes positively exotic when he has his hero wonder "if his children would constitute a sufficient engagement." One suspects that Mr. Hergesheimer is undertaking to extend the scope of English usage through the adoption of idioms from a Latin tongue; and one wonders whether he will succeed in doing so. The question presses more urgently when we read of how the hero "*disposed* his attention in a hundred channels," and of how "the tropical evening was *accomplished* rapidly."

In 1922 the favorite words of Mr. Hergesheimer are the noun "maturity" and the corresponding adjective; and while, so far as I have observed, he uses these words correctly, he certainly runs them into the ground. He gives us not merely a feeling of the juvenility of the young man who is so haunted with the notion of maturity. He gives us much the feeling that Mr. Swinnerton does with his use, well over a dozen times in his latest book, of the words "sophisticated" and "sophistication"—the feeling that he must be writing for the very young. In Havana the hero "continually found himself in situations of the most gratifying maturity—here he was in the dining-room of the Inglaterra Hotel, with a tall rum punch before him, and a mature-looking cigar." And, once started, the author does not always stop to think whether he is making sense with this continual sounding of his *leitmotif*, and he sometimes lands in humorous confusion; as where, speaking of the growing loveliness of a young woman, he says, "The *maturity of her engagement to marry* had already intensified her." One might think of the maturing of bonds, but hardly of the maturity of an engagement to marry.

Mr. Hergesheimer may be affected beyond all living novelists; but it must be acknowledged that he achieves what they all so desperately crave, and what so few of them do achieve. He is certainly "different." Mr. Scott Fitzgerald is often as affected as Mr. Hergesheimer; but the only "difference" he achieves in such passages is that of posturing affectation.

She was dazzling—alight; it was agony to comprehend her beauty in a glance. . . . . It has been very rare to have known you, very strange and wonderful. . . . . And from loving it with a vanity that was almost masculine, she became suddenly *anaesthetic* to it. . . . . Anthony pulled her quickly to her feet and held her helpless, *without breath*, in a kiss that was neither a game nor a tribute. . . . . He would drop his arm around her and *find her kiss*.

Mr. Ben Hecht is equally anxious to be different, and, like Mr. Fitzgerald, he is no doubt successful in this regard so far as conception and composition go. But in *Gargoyles*, his style, formed in a cheap school of newspaper writing, strives in vain to achieve any kind of distinction. Where he is most "subtle," most expressive in intention, he is most sadly inexpressive and common in effect. He makes a considerable use of the class of adjectives which Mr. McFee is reaching out for when he says of Mrs. Dainopoulos, "She liked Evanthia because she had that *ineluctable* quality of transfiguring an act into a grandiose gesture." That is not very bad. Apart from the use of the word "quality" for "faculty," there is no positive impropriety in the English of his sentence. But his fine word "ineluctable" is so out of place in his prosy writing that it jumps out from the page crying to be let alone. And generally Mr. McFee does leave such words alone, and so much the better for everybody concerned.

Mr. Hecht has greater pretensions to style, or to the expressive style, and he will not let these words alone. He tells us, in *Gargoyles*, that a certain woman "would snuggle kittenishly between the empty sheets, an *unintelligible* sense of immorality lending a luxury to her weariness." He seems to mean, not "unintelligible," but "vague" or "indefinable" or "curious" or "mysterious," to use the favorite words of Messrs. Swinnerton and Hutchinson in these cases. A girl tells a man, yes, she loves him. "Her 'yes' had given him an *inexplicable* moment." Why "inexplicable"? It appears simple enough. Perhaps "ineffable" is meant.

It is not in this direction that Mr. Hecht can look for distinction. Too many other authors have shared his fondness for these words. They have shared likewise his fondness for the word "sense," noun or verb, as a more precious word for feeling or feel, and have been prone, like him, to use it largely and loosely. He is not the first to speak of a heart "lacerated by the poignant things it senses," or of a man who had "inspired in him a curious sense of obedience toward all mothers he encountered." Mr. Hecht may use this word for everything, as Nona put it; but he cannot have, for his own, words which have been the favorites of every sentimental writer of the last ten years. When Mark Sabre, in

If Winter Comes, "had a sudden sense of the tremendous and poignant adventure on which they were embarked together"—he and his wife—the feeling was no doubt fresh and unique in his experience; but his author was not having any of these expressive words for his own, any more than one who rides in the loop-the-loop is having an exclusive enjoyment of that excitement. People since Pater have been having a sense of this or that, which they take for a kind of sixth sense. In the novels of Mr. Walpole, it is most likely to be a sudden sense. In Mr. Swinnerton, it is a curious or an extraordinary sense. In Mr. Wells, it has been over and over again a sense of fine adventure. In Mr. Hergesheimer and Mr. Walpole and Mr. Hutchinson and Mr. Fitzgerald and Mr. Swinnerton, as well as in Mr. Hecht, it is almost sure to be a sense of something "poignant."

It is evident that these writers aspire to a certain rarity of diction, a distinction, even a preciousness, in the use of English. And two of them, Mr. Hutchinson and Mr. Hergesheimer, have indeed a wide reputation for these very qualities. But preciousness is the privilege of writers like Stevenson and Pater and Mr. Cabell; distinction is the prerogative of writers like Thackeray and Sterne and Mr. George Moore—men who write with deliberate care and a sensitive mastery of the mother-tongue. A great outcry has been made over the commonness of Mr. Sinclair Lewis and the crudeness of Mr. Sherwood Anderson. But these men have the merit of writing plainly; and as for the King's English, they observe it with a probably greater scrupulousness than either Mr. Hutchinson or Mr. Walpole or Mr. Swinnerton.

It would take too long to illustrate the fallibility of even British writers in matters of English idiom and grammar. But some examples might be given of the figures of speech of novelists both English and American. It is probably in the use of figures that careless precious writers are most likely to betray themselves. For careless writers in general are apt to forget, what the great writers had always in mind, that figures of speech, if they are anything, are an appeal to the imagination, and that the imagination abhors being balked and cheated by a confused appeal.

When Mr. Hutchinson speaks of an "impregnably rooted impression," he forgets that "impregnably" means "not to be taken by assault," and connotes a fortress and not a root. But the reader does not forget it. When the same writer says that his lovers were "affianced as it were at a blow," no apologetic "as it were" can keep us from laughing at the violent and ludicrous image. When Mr. Hecht says of a man in love, "He was being transported," the reader remembers that to be transported means to be shipped to Tasmania for a criminal offense, and his imagination is carried far from the young man in love. When Mr. Hergesheimer says, "The simple path of truth must be put aside," we consider that paths are generally the product of much travel, and that, while they may be left at will, they are not so easily put aside. When Mr. Walpole speaks of "the pressure of her heart beating up in her throat," we image a pressure as one thing and a beating as another, and we cannot image them together. When he tells us, of a girls' party, that "a chatter arose like the murmur of bees," we feel sure that a chatter is one thing and a murmur another, and that his first impression of a girls' party is better than his second. And when he tells us that "the lamps in the High Street suddenly flaring beat out the sky," we say that that may be very fine writing, but it is not the fine writing of Ruskin or of Pierre Loti.

It is worth while to dwell a moment on the word "poignant," mentioned above. For it is the most infallible diagnostic of the disease we have under observation—a disease which we may define as the mania for indicating emotion by means of adjectives. Like the word "devastating," "poignant" is prized for suggesting emotion both strong and rare, so that the author feels himself to be writing in a manner at once vigorous and precious. It is not the word of the year, but the word of the decade, or perhaps, thus far, of the century. It makes its appeal, no doubt, to some extent because it is felt to be of Gallic origin, and as yet not quite English. It is, as a matter of fact, a good English word. You will find it used sparingly, but correctly, in Charles Lamb and Walter Scott. But somehow, among all their vices, the intervening Victorians did not number this of excessive appeal to poignancy. I doubt if the creator of Paul Dombey and Little Nell once resorted to this word for the heightening of pathos. If I remember rightly, it was not adjectives, let alone connotative and non-descriptive adjectives, with which he worked his magic. And so the word "poignant" has come down to our time a coin of sterling value. I do not know who first began to debase it. All I know is that you cannot open a sentimental novel today without encountering this now vague but fervid attributive. And the worst of it is that these emotional story-tellers, in their eagerness to be elegantly expressive, have neglected to inquire into the meaning of the word, and as often as not they use it in phrases that make no sense.

This word, however *recherché*, means simply "keen" or "piercing" or "pungent"; and the reader who has the misfortune to know its meaning is thrown into great confusion when Mr. Hutchinson, say, offers him sentences like the following, "And precisely as beauty touched him in the most exquisite and poignant depths. . . . ." Piercing depths? Pungent depths? "And Sabre would feel an immensely poignant clutch at the heart." Piercing clutch? Pungent clutch?

There we have in a word all that is most unpalatable in such writing. What we have mainly been observing is the pride of words, the affectation of a difference. Alas, one cannot achieve distinction in this manner by the adoption of half-a-dozen smart words. Smart words spread too fast. The distinction of Pater and Thackeray is more than skin deep. It is not an affair of words, but of individuality of thought and phrasing. And the worst of it is that affectation seldom walks alone. And here we have it in its characteristic combination with slovenliness and sentimental violence. It is not a combination that makes for distinction.

1923

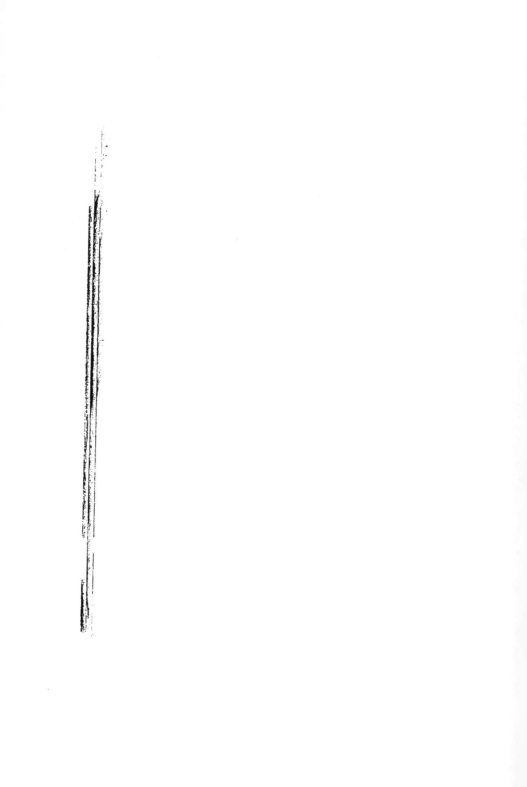

SAWING THE AIR

SAWING THE AIR

I can take off my shirt and tear it, and so make a ripping razzly noise, and the people will say: "Look at him tear his shirt."—SANDBURG.

Nor do not saw the air too much with your hand, thus, but use all gently.—SHAKESPEARE.

THE two vices of style to which current novelists are most addicted, aside from mere slovenliness, are affectation and sentimental violence. I have had my say on the subject of affectation. Affectation is bad enough. But the most suicidal practice of writers insensitive to verbal niceties is the constant, mechanical use of words, especially of adjectives and adverbs, denoting what Mr. Swinnerton so well calls "extremity of feeling." Next to "poignant," the favorite word of the moment is probably "passionate." "A passionate desire for her kisses and an equally passionate craving to hurt and mar her": the first half of the phrase might well be from an English pen; it is the "sadistic" note of the second half that marks it for the work of either Mr. Hecht or Mr. Fitzgerald. And

[125]

even the sadism is not a certain indication of American authorship; for does not Mr. Swinnerton represent the very nicest of his three lovers as "shot through and through with an impulse either to kiss or to strike her"?

In much the same class, but less common and more affected, is the word "intolerable," which Mr. Hergesheimer has brought into style among Americans, and which Mr. Swinnerton does not disdain. Not even Mr. Lewis is immune to this infection. Even his Babbitt is capable of intolerable and illogical emotions on hearing Mrs. Judique sing "My Creole Queen." But Mr. Lewis is not up to the Hergesheimer pitch. It was the hero of *Cytherea* who, with an involuntary and brutal movement, took, if I remember, the heroine in his arms, "and kissed her with a flamelike and intolerable passion." It was intolerable; but she bore it. It was flamelike; but she survived.

The trouble with this sort of thing is not that we do not like to be moved, but that this is not the way to move us. It is particularly among the English writers that the excessive use of superlatives and of repetition defeats its own purpose and wears out all our power of faith in the emotions represented. Mr. Swinnerton is not content to have his hero shot through and through with an impulse; he must

needs have his heroine shot through and through
with knowledge, and pierced through and through
with longing, and even a quiet domestic scene must
be shot through and through with a beautiful tran-
quillity. Things are not felt passionately, which in
itself implies a considerable degree of feeling; things
must be felt *most* passionately. People are not singularly, that is uniquely, moved; they must be *most*
singularly moved. The heroine must not be merely
shaken with a shudder; it must be, "A deep shudder
shook her." If there is one word in English which
tells of extreme feeling it is the word "anguish";
my dictionary calls it "excruciating distress." "Anguish" is a word which should stand out on a page
like a scarlet hunting-coat on a snowy landscape.
"Shuddering anguish" is ultra-violet, and beyond
our range of vision.

It has been suggested that some countenance is
lent to the latter-day story-tellers by the fondness of
Henry James, in such books as *The Awkward Age* and
The Golden Bowl, for adjectives like "wonderful,"
"beautiful," "magnificent." And I am inclined to
grant that certain writers have been misled by this
mannerism of James, and that much that is sentimental and affected in current writing has its ulti-
mate origin in tricks of style which in the master
are properly neither affected nor sentimental. Above

all, not sentimental. For it is obvious, on reflection, that these adjectives are not so much the property of James as of his characters, for whom they make up a sort of smart drawing-room jargon, half-humorous in tone.

And, what is still more to the point, these terms of extravagant approval are not applied to the feelings. It is by quite other means that James indicates the generally suppressed emotions of his dramatis personae. It is their social form, the intelligence with which they meet the tests applied to one another, which receives this meed of whimsical praise. It is simply the recognition these people give to the very definite moves they make in their complicated and exacting social game. To apply the term "magnificent" to the high "line" taken by Mrs. Brookenham in regard to the proposed marriage of Nanda and Van, or "beautiful" to the strategy by which Maggie wins back her husband and mends her broken bowl, is like applying the same terms to a move in chess by which one checks his opponent's king. The citation of James is the best means of exposing the crudeness of certain writers who may fancy themselves his disciples.

The least convincing and most nauseating passages in current novels are naturally the scenes of love-making. In the books of last year,[1] it is true, there was a certain abatement of what I may be allowed to call the "crushed-strawberry manner." In *The Bright Shawl* Mr. Hergesheimer has given us a book without love-making. The love-making of Joan and Johnny in *The Cathedral* is demure enough, with no reminder of the crushing embraces of the earlier works of Mr. Walpole. Mr. Hecht and Mr. Fitzgerald do indeed hark back to the physical violence of year before last. "His arms crushed her. He fastened against her. He could brook no resistance." That is from *Gargoyles*. In *The Beautiful and Damned*, it was the heroine's dress that suffered. "Together they crushed out the stiff folds of her dress in one triumphant and enduring embrace." Mr. Hutchinson rises in one passage to the requirements of sentimental passion of the arms-and-the-man type, but with a discreet avoidance of unpleasant images. The whole passage is worth citation.

> She caught her breath. . . . . .
> The thing's too poignant for the words a man has.
> She was caught in his arms, terribly enfolding her. He was crying in her ears, passionately, triumphantly, "Rosalie! Rosalie!" She was in his arms. Those long, strong arms of his were round her; and she was caught against his heart, her face upturned to his, his face against her own; and she was swoon-

[1] Note the date of writing at the end of the essay.

ing, falling through incredible spaces, drowning in incredible seas, sinking through incredible blackness; and in her ears his voice, coming to her in her extremity like the beat of a wing in the night, like the first pulsing roll of music enormously remote, "Rosalie! Rosalie!"

The thing's too poignant for the words one has.

Surely Mr. Hutchinson need not tell us more than once what we have a thousand times determined for ourselves. But what we should like him to tell us is, why, with such a conviction of the inadequacy of his words, he continues to pour them forth with such merciless copiousness. One cannot even distinguish in Mr. Hutchinson the words of this year from those of last. There is only a difference in the relative frequency of one or another. "Frightful" and "terrible" and "horrible" may turn up more frequently in last year's book; they may count up by the dozens or the scores. In this year's book the dozens or the scores are for "extraordinary," "enthralling," "enormous," and "pathetic." "Inconceivably tremendous, unimaginably awful," in last year's book gives way in this to "most terribly pathetic" and "extraordinarily wonderful and delicious"; "utterly splendid" to "tremendously splendid"; "perfectly wonderful" to "enormously wonderful." On the whole, in the later book, the same word will be found used about twice as often on a page as in the earlier.

The thoughts of Rosalie, not sequent, but going about and amounting thusly, were thus: "That is very pathetic. That is horribly sad and pathetic. Coming at the end like that and without any strokes and flourishes, it is as if she was exhausted of her hate and rage and just put out an utterly tired hand and set this here like a sigh. *That's* pathetic, the mere look of it and that thought of it. . . . . And then she steps back on his foot and there's 'his dear face' smiling at her; ah it's pathetic, it's poignant! I can see it absolutely. Yes, I can. . . . . that frightful ending of hers: 'You can get dozens and dozens of men to love you, but you have taken mine and I can never, never get another.' That is most terribly pathetic. I think that is the most poignant thing I have ever heard. Well, I can realize its utter pathos; I can realize it but I cannot feel it."

All within a page, and no end in sight!

In some parts of *This Freedom* there is just a suggestion of a very great story-teller. It was the manner of Charles Dickens, having fastened upon some droll or grotesque feature of a character, to ring the changes upon it humorous-wise in his own delicious and inimitable way, until the whole family of readers was sated with laughter. But it is with visible and substantial things that he deals, and not with adjectives; or, if with adjectives, it is not the sort of adjectives which make up the stock of Mr. Hutchinson. There is Miss Murdstone as seen by David Copperfield on her first arrival:

She brought with her two uncompromising hard black boxes, with her initials on the lid in hard brass nails. When she paid the coachman, she took her money out of a hard steel purse, and she kept the purse in a very jail of a bag which hung upon her arm by a heavy chain, and shut up like a bite. I had never, at that time, seen such a metallic lady altogether as Miss Murdstone.

There is always in Dickens a great stir and bustle like that which Mr. Hutchinson tries to create in the opening chapters of *This Freedom*. But it is a real stir and bustle, a real drollery, made up of human traits and movements caught by an artist, and not the tedious and factitious liveliness of *This Freedom*, with its endless harping on those extraordinary and wonderful males!

But, after all, the ineptitude of such writing is too gross and palpable to justify long comment. The moral of Mr. Hutchinson is for Mr. Swinnerton and Mr. Walpole. The author of *Nocturne* and *Coquette* is worth saving, and still more the author of *Fortitude* and *The Duchess of Wrexe*. And they are much in need of saving from the contagion of this manner of writing. They do not indulge in mawkish pentameters and lisping Homeric similes, like Mr. Hutchinson; they do not, like him, quote and garble the poems of Stevenson and Byron and Wordsworth (*If Winter Comes*, p. 411; *This Freedom*, pp. 151, 159); not to speak of the litany (p. 138) and the familiar rules of mathematics (p. 224). But do they realize how often they suggest the manner of their popular compatriot? They may not so often disarrange the order of English words with the self-conceit of a Roman buck wearing his toga with a difference. ("When from her first terrible dismay—that frightful crying, her face turned to the pillow—she had recovered; when to the lovely ardour of her love—stealing about her, soothing her, in the night; bursting upon her, ravishing her, in the morning—she had passed on.") But neither Mr. Walpole nor Mr. Swinnerton is altogether above the temptations of sentimental foppishness in the placing of words. "He looked across at the house as on the evening of his arrival from that same step he had looked" (*The Cathedral*). "Almost, her lips trembled. . . . . Almost, he did not look at her" (*The Three Lovers*).

And both these talented novelists have, in particular, largely gone over to the convulsive manner of indicating emotion by a series of adjectival shocks about as indicative of true feeling as the twitching features of a paralytic. I do not suppose they are deliberately imitating the style of their popular rival. I doubt if they have any idea of the habits they have fallen into. Does Mr. Swinnerton know that, in the use of the words "extraordinary" and "extraordinarily," he has exceeded in his last book the average frequency of Mr. Wells, and actually approaches the figures of Mr. Hutchinson? Does Mr. Walpole know how often, in his wish to make us realize the suffering of his characters, he uses the words "horrible" and "horror," "terrible" and "terribly," "desperate" and "desperately"? Does either of them realize how often, in the effort to make us jump with their characters, they jab us with the words "sudden" and "suddenly," until we grow hard skin over that sensitive spot? "Suddenly an absurd fancy seized her. . . . . Then suddenly it overcame her. . . . . He suddenly smiled. . . . . She suddenly realized. . . . . 'Love me!' he burst out suddenly, starting up in his chair. . . . . He turned, looking at her. Then suddenly put his arms around her and kissed her." All in less than two pages. This happens to be from *The Cathedral*, but it might just as well be from *The Three Lovers*.

It is in passages where they would render the sensations of a character with a weak or agitated heart that these men most remind us of Mr. Hutchinson. I have seldom met with a person in fiction who was so liable as Patricia Quin to racing, beating, and fluttering of the heart—a person, that is, who is supposed to possess a sound organ. Mr. Walpole has more occasion for registering such phenomena, inasmuch as he is preparing the reader for the eventual death of Archdeacon Brandon. But Mr. Walpole might have given us quite sufficient warning of that event with a third or a quarter of his display of medical science. The thing begins to get ridiculous long before we come to the death of the archdeacon. The climax comes when the author assures us, in a most serious passage, that "Brandon's heart began to race round like a pony in a paddock." It is this kind of thing that makes one feel in reading *The Cathedral* and *The Three Lovers* that one is dealing with hackwork, turned out by the yard—the sort of thing they do in Hollywood and Carmel-by-the-Sea.

This is in no sense the style of the great dramatic writers. It is the refuge of those who feel not deeply but too well. Archdeacon Brandon is well conceived, and obviously of the kindred of Michael Henchard, the Casterbridge grain-merchant and his own worst enemy. Let Mr. Walpole read again his *Mayor of Casterbridge*. Mr. Walpole is evidently a disciple of Dostoevsky, who writes so profoundly of the spiritual history of "our town." Let him read *The Brothers Karamazov*. Let him read *Anna Karénina*. He and Mr. Swinnerton wish to represent the mental sufferings of human beings strongly endowed. Let them read of the insomnia of Evelyn Innes, which drove her into the convent, or of Esther Waters awaiting the news from the Derby which was to settle the fate of her husband—life or death. The great writers deal not in adjectives, the words of the year; they deal "boldly with substantial things."

Oh, that I had the brush of Max Beerbohm! Oh, that I had his pen, that I might show these men, in parody, the folly of their ways! But the author of *A Christmas Garland* has woven a wreath for distinguished brows. It is men of note whom he celebrates with parody—John Galsworthy and Joseph Conrad, Maurice Hewlett and Hilaire Belloc. Let the younger men choose their company, let them choose their models well, lest they may never be game for such as Max Beerbohm.

1923

THE PEACOCK'S TAIL

THE PEACOCK'S TAIL

THE greatest passion of civilized humanity is to be right in matters of taste. In art the great thing is to put your money on the right horse. Not necessarily the horse that is bound to win. It is a long view from start to finish of the race, and it is more important to pick the favorite of the moment than to pocket your money at the end. The figure of your money is a poor one, since in questions of taste there is nothing to lose but an opinion and in matters of opinion our memories are short. In Mr. Carl Van Vechten's *Blind Bow-Boy* (August, 1923) the man of most advanced taste remarks that " everything one called modern a year or two ago is old fashioned"; and he proceeds to give a long list of the names on which the author put his money in *Peter Whiffle* (April, 1922). Who reads *Peter Whiffle* now? In 1922 he might make his reputation for modernity with Mary Garden and Marcel Proust. In 1923 he must proceed to Honegger and Ronald Firbank. In matters of taste " good" and "up to date" are interchangeable terms.

Everything depends, of course, on one's milieu. Arthur Machen has reached Madison. Jacques Copeau has reached Los Angeles. In Kansas City it is permissible to admire Van Dyke. In London, where they keep Van Dyke, it is better form to admire Van Gogh. Mr. George Moore continues to think he did well in the early days to acquire certain exemplars of Edouard Manet; they will tell him in Washington Square that he would have done better to choose Cézanne.

There are still people with long memories, people who like to pick the winner not of this year but of a decade. And there is of course that strange inversion of ideals by which in academic circles men pride themselves on admiring only the old. I have been told by a distinguished professor of poetry that he never reads any verse later than 1850. And he is an editor of Poe, and what in the university world we call "a modern man." I know many professors who never read any verse since Chaucer nor any prose since Dryden. But all this is but another indication of how much, in the universities, they are out of sympathy with the spirit of the times. The spirit of the times is an indiscriminate passion for the *dernier cri*.

And to any reader truly impregnated with the spirit of the times I have no hesitation in cordially recommending Mr. Carl Van Vechten as being, at least on New Year's, 1925, absolutely the *dernier cri*, so far as it can be had—or heard—in English. *The Tiger in the House* I cannot recommend. It is an amusing and instructive collection of information about cats; but there is nothing modern about it except the pictures. It might have been compiled by an industrious German scholar; and I am not sure but what, in great part, it was. As for the critical works of 1920 or earlier, the reader would not be interested in anything so antiquated. It is true that several of them are out of print—in itself a recommendation to the bibliophile. But *The Tattooed Countess* and *The Blind Bow-Boy* I can recommend without reservation; and for the discriminating reader even *Peter Whiffle*, providing he will bear in mind that it is three years old.

Mr. Van Vechten is the Baedeker of the intelligentsia. His novels are veritable guidebooks to Paris and New York, with the stars on everything that Baedeker leaves undistinguished and E. V. Lucas ignores. In *Peter Whiffle* he devotes many solid pages to a list of the things he did in Paris during his visit there in his twenties. He concludes with the modest declaration: "In short, you will observe that I did everything that young Americans do when they go to Paris." It is a very modest declara-

tion. What he means is that he did very much more
than other young Americans do, having inside information, and that other young Americans will do
well to profit by his suggestions. "I dined with
Olive Fremstad at the Mercedes and Olive Fremstad
dined with me at the Café d'Harcourt." Not all
young Americans will be in a position to invite distinguished opera-singers to dinner, let alone being
invited to dine with them. But they can look up the
Mercedes or the Café d'Harcourt and invite to dinner whatever most distinguished friend they find in
Paris. They can follow Mr. Van Vechten to lunch
at the Deux Magots in the company of unidentified
artists presided over by the two bland grotesques.
They can learn from him where to get their perfum-
ery and dresses, if they are women; what bars and
music halls to frequent, if they are men; where, in
either case, to find Brittany china-ware and impres-
sionist paintings. They can learn to speak easily of
Dranem and Max Dearly, André Gide and Jeanne
Bloch.

In the later chapters of *Peter Whiffle*, Mr. Van
Vechten does much the same things for New York,
and in *The Blind Bow-Boy* again, the scene is New
York. It is true that the leading character is an
English duke who talks French, and whose talk
is "of Capri, from whence the Duke had recently

emerged, the new English plays, Poiret's inventions for the grues at Auteuil, Cocteau's café, and kindred subjects." The cultural specialty of the book is perhaps the many detailed descriptions of interiors anything but banal in decoration; the reader has but to turn the leaves to learn what pictures and bibelots are the last word for the salon of a lady, the bedroom of a duke, or the boudoir of a kept (a very well-kept!) woman.

Unfortunately, *The Tattooed Countess* does not share in this kind of interest. We hardly need a Baedeker for Maple Valley, Iowa, and if we did, the need has been amply supplied by Mr. Floyd Dell. The Countess Nattatorrini arrived in Maple Valley in the now uninteresting year of 1897, and if she brought with her remembrances of Italy and Paris and London, they referred to matters which are now but ancient history, like the New York of Mrs. Wharton's archaizing novels or Mr. Hergesheimer's Philadelphia and Salem. The novelty of *The Tattooed Countess* lies solely in the words—a subject to which I shall come in due course, after a little further consideration of Mr. Van Vechten's discoveries in the world of art.

The reader who likes to be "in the know"—and who of us is exempt from this pardonable, nay, this intellectual aspiration?—must perforce be grateful to Mr. Van Vechten for his useful hints. It may seem ungracious to suggest that the thing is overdone. But indeed it does smack a bit of ostentation. Our author seems in such a hurry to pluck his flowers, to bring in his armful of novelties, as if he feared that someone might get ahead of him. He is so much concerned to avoid the commonplace, to deal solely in the caviare. He loses no opportunity to present a list of things—of pictures, music, books. He catalogues the libraries of his friends. He reminds us of the hostess who gives to the newspapers a complete list of her guests.

There is a passion for things of the mind, and there is another passion for being in the know. Most widespread of all ambitions of young men is the ambition to order the right drinks. One is reminded in some of Mr. Van Vechten's cultural flights of the passage—itself, for that matter, a cultural flight—in which he tells us of his exploits at the Café de la Paix.

It had become my custom to pass two hours of every afternoon on this busy corner, first ordering tea with two brioches, and later a succession of absinthes, which I drank with sugar and water. In time I learned to do without the sugar, just as eventually I might have learned to do without the water, had I not learned to do without the absinthe. I was enjoying my third pernod while my companions were dallying with whisky and soda.

It is comforting to think that it was not the alcohol that attracted Peter Whiffle's friend so much as the sense of being right in a matter of taste.

In literary theory and in his own practice Mr. Van Vechten displays the same passion for the last word of modernity. The word which he finds is the word "sophistication," and the evidence of sophistication is, in his view, a light, ironic manner. In *The Blind Bow-Boy* the mouthpiece of his ideals is a New York society woman who for all feeling and for all sentiment seems to have substituted a lively set of opinions on aesthetics. She has, for one thing, no patience with the heavy manner of Waldo Frank and Theodore Dreiser.

Why, she wondered, did authors write in this uncivilized and unsophisticated manner? How was it possible to read an author who never laughed? For it was only behind laughter that true tragedy could lie concealed, only the ironic author who could awaken the deeper emotions. The tragedies of life, she reflected, were either ridiculous or sordid. The only way to get the sense of this absurd, contradictory, and perverse existence into a book was to withdraw entirely from the reality. The artist who feels most poignantly the bitterness of life wears a persistent and sardonic smile. She remembered the salubrious remark of a character in André Salmon's *La Négresse du Sacré Cœur:* There is only one truth, steadfast, healing, salutary, and that is the absurd.

What, indeed, could be more up to the minute than such sophistication, such disillusion, such a sense of the tragic futility of life? It is particularly prevailing, particularly natural, in war-disordered Europe. One cannot read such books as *La Négresse du Sacré-Cœur* or Paul Morand's *Fermé la Nuit* without receiving a dismal impression of a world bewildered, in which not merely destiny but even man is without aim, without hope, without values. One receives the same impression from a show of paintings in which the artists have deliberately renounced all charm of line, all splendor of color and light, from a concert of music made up of nervous jerks and snarls and ending forever off key in a whimpering question. There is a certain character to much of this work, a deal of ingenuity and erudition, and it seems indeed the sincere expression of a characteristic view of life. It is the art of our time in Europe, and as such must be respected.

The trouble is that it has, at the same time, a sort of market value as being the last word. And thousands of artists who have no color of their own make it their pride to take the color, the latest color, of the time. Particularly in America, where the sort of thing is not at home, it has often a factitious and apelike bearing. It seems to say, "Behold me! have I not divested myself completely of the old sweetness and the old simplicity? Can you not sense the heartbreak and disillusion behind my mask of gaiety?"

And we cannot always give the answer demanded. Sophistication, if that be something to be desired, is a state of mind implying a process of thought and initiation; it is a philosophical makeshift, a *pis-aller*. Disillusion is a *modus vivendi* of idealists whose ideals have suffered damage; it implies a depth of feeling, a seriousness of aspiration.

Mr. Van Vechten admires *La Négresse du Sacré-Cœur*, from which he has taken, one suspects, some suggestions for drawing the nude, and he quotes, somewhat inaccurately, certain remarks of the writer of Montmartre. He has not given us anywhere the equivalent of the actual tragedy which inspired the remarks of Florimond Daubelle. Nor of the German, suspected of being a spy, who brought up the body of little Léontine from the pit where she had thrown herself. "He looked not on the crowd nor on the sky but on something that is not of these lands nor of the country yonder, something which is between earth and sky and which a very few men begin to perceive, if they are very brave and persevering." Mr. Van Vechten admires Aldous Huxley, ironic and sophisticated, but he has not given us tragedy like that of the painter Phillotson in "Mortal Coils" who outlived his own fame, nor that of the dwarfs in *Crome Yellow* who were put to shame by their giant offspring. He admires Mr.

Cabell, amusing and ironic, but he does not realize perhaps that *Jurgen* and *Figures of Earth* are the history of souls aspiring, and sophisticated in their own despite, flames "wind-driven but aspiring," as Meredith says of Diana. He admires the witty master of all ironists, Anatole France. But does he realize the gravity of the *Isle of Penguins*, of *Thaïs?* The characters of Anatole France, by the way, are never sophisticated, like Campaspe Lorillard. Terribly earnest is Thaïs, the apostle of love, and Paphnuce, apostle of asceticism, and all the philosophers of that amazing Egyptian banquet. If there is any sophistication in Anatole France, it is the net result of his long dealings with matters the most serious to the human heart and head.

"How could anything serious be hidden more successfully," thinks Campaspe Lorillard, "than in a book which pretended to be light and gay?" In Mr. Van Vechten's books the serious things are certainly well hidden. An amusing creation is Peter Whiffle, this runaway from Toledo, who has exhausted all the force of his will in escaping from the mediocrity of his father's bank and espousing vaguely the life of art; this irresolute artist who can never make up his mind on any question, and who drifts from one absurd theory of writing to another without ever putting any into practice. But he does not seem to stand for anything more significant than futility in the abstract. It might be supposed at times that it is all intended for a satire on the type of writing represented by Mr. Van Vechten, only it is too evident that his creator shares with him his enthusiasm for literary ideals out of the common road, no matter what, so long as they are surprising and not shared by the vulgar.

The Blind Bow-Boy appears to be intended for a study in disillusion. But disillusion implies the loss of ideals, and Harold Prewett is not known to have had any ideals to lose. The story serves actually as an occasion for the author to parade such figures as Campaspe and the Duke of Middlebottom—people whose aim in life is to seek out new gratifications for their aesthetic vanity. One remembers the words of Flaubert: "I seek new perfumes, larger flowers, pleasures untried." But there is none of the holy passion of Flaubert in these lives; there is little but the complacency of Flaubert's contemporaries whose aim in life was to shock their neighbors, *épater les bourgeois*. And they and their discovery, the child of nature, Zimbule O'Grady, give the author his opportunity to shock the bourgeois a little on his own account—an exercise which, for the rest, has now at last its market value in America.

It is clear from many indications that the great

models of Mr. Van Vechten are George Moore (of the *Confessions of a Young Man*) and Huysmans (of *À Rebours*)—men who so loved to swim against the current of their time. It is a bit ironic, indeed, to consider that, of this author so proud of bringing us ever the last word in the arts, they should say now on the rue de l'Odéon that, compared with Waldo Frank, he is old style, still walking in the track of *À Rebours*. *À Rebours* is verily the Bible of those who follow the cult of the rare, of the *au delà de l'art*. But we find in Van Vechten none of the heat and depth of feeling of the hero Des Esseintes, who, when he had to return to vulgar Paris from his aristocratic seclusion, addressed his fervent prayer to a god in whom he did not believe. "Lord, take pity on the Christian who doubts, on the unbeliever who longs to believe, on the convict of life who embarks alone, in the night, under a firmament no longer lighted by the consoling lanterns of the old hope!" We know that, beneath the crust of vanity, of snobbishness, there was in Huysmans the profound love of a cultivated man for whatever is rare, the patience and tenacity of a scholar, and the desperation of a man bent on saving his soul, who in the end did save it in the one way he could conceive.

In his American disciple we tap the crust of

vanity in anxious and uncertain hopes of finding something solid underneath.

As for the disciple of George Moore, we should acclaim him with enthusiasm if he gave promise of some day presenting us with an *Esther Waters* or an *Evelyn Innes*. We should even give him a high place as an English stylist if he would show us pages written like any page in the *Confessions*. Already in those early days Mr. Moore had achieved a style strong, supple, and above all simple. He was already an English purist of the school of Oscar Wilde —another of Mr. Van Vechten's admirations. It was from the best French models that these men learned to write such impeccable English, in a classic manner worthy of Congreve and Addison. Very different is the ideal of Mr. Van Vechten as set forth in the Preface to *Peter Whiffle*. In this testamentary letter to his friend Van Vechten, Peter Whiffle explained how difficult it was to recover the lucid moments of vision when he was potentially an author. "To recapture them I should have been compelled to invent a new style, *a style capricious and vibratory* as the moments themselves. In this, however, as you know, I have failed, while you have succeeded." It is perhaps a pardonable vanity on the part of the author to claim for himself a success which has been so generally accorded him by the critics. London and New York unite to grant him, as his dominant quality, glitter, and New York has added the revealing judgment that "he has some very happy hits in verbal virtuosity."

The phrase is most appropriate, reproducing so well in its alliterative and slightly facetious turn some of the means by which Mr. Van Vechten produces his effect of glitter. He is, for one thing, a diligent collector of rare words from the most out-of-the-way places, and his pages sparkle with outlandish terms as the diadem of an actress sparkles with apocryphal gems: "koprologniac tastes," "adscititious qualities," "fragrant acervation," "dehiscent jaw," "pimpant and steatopygous figures," "pinguid and amblyoptic gentlemen." There is, to be sure, nothing new in this. It has long been a recognized device of humorous writing in English—not the humor of Swift or of Max Beerhohm—to provoke the reader's smile by saying simple things in elephantine periphrasis. And Mr. Van Vechten is fond of the sort of wit which consists in saying "paronomasia" where he means a play on words, "vocatively adjured" where he means severely prohibited, "impinging on her consciousness" where he means coming into her mind, and "a feline death scene" where he means the death of a cat.

But such individual flowers of rhetoric give but

an inadequate idea of the quality of his style when he is most conscious of the call for verbal virtuosity. This can best be suggested by more extended passages of lively writing.

> *Completely confident* by now that his father was *certainly* more terrified than he had been at any *stage* of *this strange game*, Harold *grew steadily* cooler. He *stared* at the rows of books in *shelves* . . . . and then he ventured *to look back* at this eccentric figure who seemed *to be ostentatiously pretending to be unaware of his presence.*

If I have failed to italicize any words it is not that any of them fail to illustrate one trick or another of this capricious and vibratory style. A captious reader might complain of such an intemperate use of alliteration as passing the bounds of discreet humor and verging on the burlesque. He will open the book at random and come upon phrases like this, "moodily occupied with such morbid meditations," and sentences like this, "These wasters, apparently, incessantly staggered about seeking sensation." And a reader versed in the virtuosity of Meredith or Lamb is inclined to wonder whether he should not attribute to the awkwardness rather than the cleverness of the author these jaw-breaking series of adverbs, "apparently incessantly staggered," "a particularly ornately constructed sofa"; these staggering series of infinitive phrases, "to look back at this

figure who seemed to be pretending to be unaware,"
"to get on sufficiently well to enable him to support
his wife."

A writer less enamored of the capricious style
would have asked himself whether there was no
way to avoid these awkward combinations. And he
would have seen at once that, in avoiding the awkwardness he might at the same time contribute to
the lucidity and forcefulness of his writing. George
Moore would never have said, "to get on sufficiently
well to enable him to support his wife." He would
have said simply, "to get on sufficiently well to support his wife." Oscar Wilde would never have said,
"completely confident that his father was certainly
more terrified," but simply "confident that his
father was more terrified." It would be to say everything that Mr. Van Vechten says and to spare us
both of the offending adverbs.

It is not fashionable in our day, and it may be
thought pedantic, to point out the habitual misuse
of English in popular writers. But when it is a question of an author who has a reputation for style, it
might be a consideration of real value in determining whether his reputation is deserved. The unit of
musical excellence is the musical phrase. The unit
of excellence in English style is the English word.
When I find myself bewildered by a new painter or

a new composer—he has a certain vogue among lovers of the up to date; he interests me by the novelty of his formula; but his formula is certainly not that of Degas or that of Haydn—I find it natural, first of all, to consult those who have a technical knowledge of the art in question. This painter, whatever his formula, does he know how to paint? This composer, does he know music? And when I receive an affirmative answer, I am prepared to look again, to listen once more, and to give the benefit of the doubt to a Darius Milhaud or a Severini. But when the answer is negative, I am more inclined to question the formula, to doubt whether the pretensions of this artist are not bogus ones. How can his novelties be worth while if he does not know how to paint, or to put together the elements of music?

And so when I find myself inclined to question the formula of Mr. Van Vechten, when I am in doubt how much to allow for certain amusing inventions in an author who strikes me as rather flashy, I say it may be helpful to take into consideration the elementary features of style. And it seems to me not without significance that he is constantly misusing English words; that he uses "betray" when he means "discover" ("Only once did Harold *betray* what he thought was a trace of affectation in the Duke"); that he uses "withal" when he means

"although" ("*withal* this taste was somewhat bizarre"); "communication" where he means "com-
munion" ("He held daily *communication* with himself"); "aggrandize" where he means "increase"
("a suspicion which seemed to *aggrandize* with every
new opportunity"); and "scantily" where he means
"hardly" or "slightly" (a man "*scantily* past
thirty," i.e., insufficiently past thirty—when was
ever man insufficiently past thirty?); and that all
this he does in one of the latest of his many published works, and one that represents presumably
the maturity of his style. And it seems not without
significance, too, that these slips are generally made
in the use of words a bit archaic, or rare, or otherwise showy, as where, again, he says of the duke
that he "seemed free from a mania for exhibitionism." He means simply "exhibitionism," or a mania
for making a show of himself. But "exhibitionism"
is a somewhat technical word, and the author betrays himself a little in his mania for verbal virtuosity.

But there is always, one says, the glitter. And
one thinks of Meredith; one thinks of Anatole
France. One is prepared for the pointed phrase, the
flashing figure of speech, sharp as a sword, the amusing paradox, the intellectual illumination. Here at
least, one says, there will be no truce with *cliché*, no

compromise with the banal, no drab and messy figures, no flavor of the bromide. And one opens the
book on such gems as these: "Friendship, indeed, is
as perilous a relationship as marriage; it, too, entails
responsibility, that great god whose existence bur-
dens our lives"; where the precious stone of thought
is so innocent of the cutter's tool, so little disen-
gaged from its native ore. Or such an epigram as
this: "I think it is Oscar Wilde who has written,
only mediocre minds are consistent. There is something very profound in this aphorism." I find it
hard to believe that Oscar Wilde should ever have
let go so flat and unfashioned a saying. Perhaps Mr.
Van Vechten is thinking of Emerson's more pointed
version: "With consistency great souls have nothing to do."

Mr. Van Vechten devotes more than one chapter
of his history of Peter Whiffle to an account of his
own travels in France. It is perhaps to give us sentences like this:

The trip across England—I had landed at Liverpool—and
the horrid channel, I will not describe, although both made
sufficient impression on me, but the French houses at Dieppe
awakened my first deep emotion and then, and so many times
since, the Normandy cider, quaffed in a little café, conter-
minous to the railroad, and the journey through France, alive
in the sunlight, for it was May, the fields dancing with the
green grain spattered with vermilion poppies and cerulean

cornflowers, the white roads, flying like ribbons between the stately poplars, leading away over the charming hills past the red-brick villas, completed the siege of my not too easily given heart.

It is a long sentence, with much in it to provoke thought. And, first of all, one is surprised to think of the number of times it was necessary for the cider and the journey to complete the siege of this difficult heart. And then one thinks of certain pages of Stevenson, of Pater, of George Moore, and of the French landscape as it appears in them. Then one thinks of the patient search for the *mot juste* by the great masters of prose in French and English. One scans again these "white roads, flying like ribbons between the stately poplars," these "fields dancing with the green grain spattered with vermilion poppies and cerulean cornflowers." And one wonders whether, if this be not actually the last word of modern style, it may not be perhaps the "limit" of the banal.

No, Mr. Van Vechten does not reach the limit of the banal until in *The Tattooed Countess* he essays a subject in itself without distinction, and applies to it, not the vocabulary of George Moore writing the history of Esther Waters, but, literally, the vocabulary of Maple Valley. The gala entertainment given in Hall's Opera House in honor of the returned countess is described in just the vein of sophomoric burlesque which might have been employed by a young man of Maple Valley recently back from college. And throughout the book the diction and syntax are indistinguishable from that prevailing among educated midwesterners, except for the frequent intrusion of big words familiar to those only who have made a special study of the dictionary. Generally speaking, there is no suggestion of a humorous intention, but since there is almost invariably some more familiar word available in the context, the effect is to show the author himself in a somewhat humorous light. In the following passage of my own invention I have collected some of the more striking words and locutions, in order to give in essence the general effect of this style of writing. Whatever attracts attention by its strangeness is taken direct from the pages of *The Tattooed Countess;* I have done nothing but weave together these bizarreries into a connected pattern of discourse. !

The pinguid countess was sitting on her porch, vainly endeavoring to overcome her egrimony by watching the procession of inhabitants of Maple Valley passing down Main Street. Suddenly she noticed a carious and otiose carriage—a buggy, in fact—which so nearly resembled the vehicle in which she drove from Sorrento to Amalfi with her dear Cecco that it only increased the epithumetic, not to say emetic, quality of her mood. Quite as suddenly it passed out of sight, drawn by its scrawny and sciapodous horse, and there was nothing left but the procacious sparrows, hopping about on the grass, and causing the dry twigs to crepitate in a way that filled her with a sense of impending doom. She remembered that the sparrow is Venus's bird, and not wishing to be a mere sciolist, she decided to call them precocious. That was evidently no more than the truth when you considered the enormous number of them in this one family; and this only emphasized her own inappetency in so far as regarded sexual emotion or any enjoyment that she might have profited by in her home town. They were of that species that show a striated wing, being strongly imbued with the protective coloration of the town, and she saw no excuse for God having created any creature as helpless as herself. Suddenly she remembered that cyanide of potassium is a painless method of taking one's own life. She discarded the cigarette which she had been subconsciously smoking, and started to enter the house. But just at that moment her sister Dinah came out the front door, and the countess quite suddenly made up her mind that here if ever was a chance for morigeration. With a fastuous, considering all the elements of the situation, air of finality, she said to her sister, "Why don't you stay in the house and mind your own business?"

And so I went to take counsel of the Deux Magots where they sit enthroned in the café opposite the church of Saint-Germain-des-Prés. It was New Year's Eve, and all the world had come to read the countenance of our new master as he made his entry in the rain. The Wise Men from the East sat with ordered skirts and with grave, calm faces, untroubled by the tragedy or the absurdity of life. Slowly they spoke, deliberately, and with long intervals of meditative silence. And first he of the turban and the rosary made himself heard, his face seeming to brighten as he spoke:

"What then is new and what is old?" he said. "The truth is a phoenix, and newborn every day."

And the other Wise Man spoke, he with his hands spread open toward the boulevard. "The Temple," he said, "was not built in a night."

And the first Wise Man spoke again. "Vanity," he said, "is not the shadow of pride. Without the substance there can be no shadow. Where is no pride," he said, "vanity takes its place in the heart."

And the other Wise Man spoke again, and it was the last of the words of wisdom, "Each new year a new peacock spreads his tail on the steps of the Temple."

And the New Year made his entry in the rain.

JANUARY, 1925

ENGLISH SPEECH AND AMERI-
CAN MASTERS

ENGLISH SPEECH AND AMERI-
CAN MASTERS

I remember watching Conrad dig his hands fiercely into the loose sand, and say, "Ah, if only I could write zee English good, well. But you see, you will see!" . . . . There is a foreign inflexion in his speech, never in his prose. . . . . And my young literary friends call him Master.—C. Lewis Hind, *Authors and I.*

AN anxious problem confronts the lover of the English language these days in the shape of many of our most interesting novels. Can we admit among reputable works of literary art stories so badly written? Can we admit to the company of Fielding and Thackeray, of Hawthorne and Jane Austen, even of Dickens, writers who at every turn offend our ears with speech not English? We are ready enough to take seriously a writer who takes himself as seriously as Mr. Dreiser; we might be a trifle readier if he were a trifle less serious. We recognize, at any rate, the scientific spirit in which he undertakes his studies of Philadelphia finance or the Chicago saloon—realizing them as American institutions. But we have come to expect that great works of fiction should be at least decently written. And it gives us a shock to find the ambitious author of *Sister Carrie* falling continually into vulgarisms like "equally well as" and "He *saw where* a new play was at the Casino."

Mr. Hergesheimer is one of the authors for whose next story we look with most excitement. We freely acknowledge him as our cleverest entertainer, our most colorful and inventive designer of patterns in the stuff of life. We are forever on the point of yielding ourselves up without reserve to the charm, the wizardry, of his romantic confections. But we are forever being brought up sharp, even in so late a book as *Linda Condon*, by the evidence that he has not mastered the rudiments of English idiom or of universal rhetoric. Nowhere does a language display its idiosyncrasy more surely than in the use of prepositions; and we find Mr. Hergesheimer groping helplessly among our "withs" and "bys" and "ats" and "ins." He does not seem aware of the fact that we make the pronoun agree in number with its antecedent ("If she didn't . . . . pay the bills every three months when *it* arrived . . . ."); that we use different pronouns for persons and things (example below); or of a dozen other facts of grammar which every schoolboy knows. He seems fond of a debonair indeterminateness of grammar, as in the sentence, "The gesture of her hands and lifted eyebrows *were* keenly expressive. . . . . ." As for what I call "universal rhetoric," what shall we say to such a change of horses in midstream—not to mention anything else—as in the following not untypical sentence? "Lithe actresses in a revealing severity of attire, like spoiled nuns with carmine lips, suffering in ingenuous problems of the passions, agonized in shuddering tones; or else *they* went to concerts to hear young violinists, slender, with intense faces and dramatic hair, play concertos, that irritated Linda with little shivers of delight."

This is not the way the old masters wrote English. Must we think of Mrs. Wharton and Mr. Cabell, as well as Mr. George Moore, as benighted Victorians because they never make these "breaks"? And which shall we feel worse about, the bad grammar or the lame rhetoric? The one betrays unprivileged birth, but the other betrays careless thinking. Mr. Hardy was not of privileged birth; and so it came about that the greatest English novelist of his day could occasionally—oh, rarely!—lapse into a vulgar idiom ("There was an uneasiness in recognizing *such*"); and could sadly misquote, through colloquial ignorance, an exquisite English poet ("I *sat* her on my pacing steed"). But Mr. Hardy almost invariably says what he means, and what he says invariably makes sense; whereas the irritating thing about many current novelists is that, through defect of rhetoric, they are constantly saying something different from what they mean, if not positively without meaning. It is of course seldom that even Mr. Dreiser makes a bull like this: "He *breakfasted* as poorly as the night before." (If one breakfasts late at night, one surely omits the function altogether on the morning after!) And there is little harm in that, except that it makes us laugh in the wrong place. But much more frequent and fatal are the knots in which Mr. Hergesheimer ties himself up, largely through excessive cleverness. Mere theoretical blunders I pass over, misplaced modifiers and necessary words left out. But what intimate faculty of logic has gone wrong for the production of the following? Referring to women and a certain man—"In reality he could offer them no help; their problems—in a world created more objectively by the hand of man than God—were singular to themselves." I have never been able to make out what, in that sentence, is the matter with God, or how he came there.

The slovenliness is obvious. But what is the matter at bottom is affectation. Half the vulgar errors of Mr. Dreiser in his earlier novels come from his pretentiousness, the way he tries to decorate his page with odds and ends suitable, if rightly used, to

Indiana oratory of the eighties. It is this which leads him to speak of something as descending upon somebody "without his *let or hindrance*," confusing, in the interests of fine writing, the opposed meanings of the word "let"; of someone's being "received without *equivocation* as a friend and equal" (meaning without cavil or question); of poisons that "*inveigh against* the system" (meaning injure); and so on with many another word too tough for his digestion. The affectations of Mr. Hergesheimer are much smarter, and harder to illustrate in small space. It is easy to instance the "utters" and "utterlys" that prove so irritating to a placid reader of the earlier books. It is härder to exemplify, or even define, the more offensive affectations in a book like *Linda Condon*, though they infect the whole air of certain passages like the smell of cheap perfume at a matinée. Mr. Hergesheimer likes to take on words and tricks of expression which he feels to be subtle or "strong" or *recherché*—large vague words, large vague connections of thought (a caricature of Henry James or May Sinclair), which are doubtless supposed, like the flannels and soft collar of his sculptor Playdon, to suit "the largeness of his being and gestures." He imagines he is enlarging the scope of expression in English. What is most offensive of all is the air of nonchalance with which he per-

petrates his barbarities, the insolent parade of carelessness.

In spite of her shrinking, of a half articulate appeal, he
crushed her against his face. Whatever that [*sic*] had filled
her with hope, she thought, was being torn from her. A sick-
ening aversion over which she had no control made her stark
in his arms. The memories of the *painted coarse satiety* of women
and the sly hard men for *which* they schemed, the loose discus-
sions [construction?] of calculated advances and sordid sur-
renders, flooded her with a *loathing for what she passionately
needed* to be beautiful.

It must be reluctantly acknowledged that such
writing is commoner in American than in English
novels. The Swinnertons and the Walpoles are more
discreet in their affectations and more nearly im-
maculate in their rhetoric. Mr. Lawrence is seldom
guilty of worse than clumsiness. With these writers the style is almost worthy of the idea and the
architectural design to which it is applied. The English of Miss Richardson and Miss Sidgwick is more
than adequate to their fine intentions. So that we
begin to wonder whether it is not simply our inferior culture that is to blame for the untidy appearance so many of our writers present to the world
—is it simply that our Dreisers and our Hergesheim-
ers are not born to the use of English, and that
Indiana and Pennsylvania have failed to supply the
deficiency?

Some color is given to this supposition by the one notable exception, among the novelists of England, to their adequate mastery of English. The most splendid of all their inventors, the boldest and surest of all their masters of technique, is the one who offends most often against the proprieties of English speech; and he was, we cannot forget, no Englishman at all, not even a native of England, but one born to the use of a Slavic tongue, who often seems to come at his acquired English by way of his acquired French. It is true that the linguistic accomplishment of Mr. Conrad is one of the seven wonders of our time; but for all that, and in spite of the opinion of Mr. Hind, one has but to read a few pages in almost any of his novels to learn that he is far from having mastered all the niceties of our idiom. There is, for example, our way of expressing possibility in a subordinate clause after a past tense, hard enough for all foreigners: "It occurred to Captain Mitchell that his position *could* [might] become disagreeable." "It did not matter what that man *would* [might] say or do." It is indeed amusing to watch out, in Conrad, for words and idioms which are direct transferences from the French: "deception" in the sense of "disillusionment"; "I did my possible" (*J'ai fait mon possible*); "I felt like a chill grip . . . ." (*comme*).

But here is just the point where the analogy breaks down. Mr. Conrad makes mistakes in English simply from the ignorance of a foreigner. It is not, like Mr. Dreiser, from bad taste, from taking for model the style of Robert G. Ingersoll: "The mystic chords which bind and thrill the heart of the nation. . . . ." (Chords *thrill*, surely, but it is *cords* that bind, as Mr. Dreiser shows us in another passage of similar sentiment: "The mystic cords of affection! How they bind us all.") Mr. Conrad never, like Mr. Hergesheimer, affects the careless style of one putting upon the page unaltered the jottings of his notebook by way of being "impressionistic." Nor do we ever find in Conrad a (psychological?) jargon like this: "The movement, the anxiety, she dreaded was arriving, and it found her no freer of doubt than had the other aspects of her own responses."

Bad taste is indeed as much as bad grammar one of the symptoms of inferior culture. But bad taste is one of those crimes for which you cannot indict a nation; and we have too many honorable exceptions to the prevalence of this sort of bad taste for us to run into hasty generalization; we have, for example, the writing of Miss Cather—from Nebraska—and that of Mr. Dell—from Illinois. So the case reduces itself to one of individuals. But unfortunately the individuals concerned are sometimes persons of account; and the better taste of Miss Cather and Mr. Dell would give us more comfort if we felt certain they were writers of equal force with Mr. Dreiser and Mr. Hergesheimer. That is why our problem is an anxious one. Mr. Hergesheimer, in particular, is likely to cause many a sleepless night to those of us who take the art of fiction seriously. We should like to hail his books as masterpieces; we came near doing so with *Java Head* and *The Three Black Pennys*. But how can we hail as American masterpieces works not written in the language of these states?

1921

THE NAÏVE STYLE

THE NAÏVE STYLE

ONE of the saddest circumstances involved in the birth of literature is that so many writers equipped for saying things well have nothing to say, whereas a large proportion of those with most interesting things to say have only the most rudimentary sense of how to say them. They have not the art or the instinct for conveying ideas in the medium of words. They are, so far as expression is concerned, in the naïve, or uninstructed, state of mind. So that, while we have a large body of excellent writing which nobody wants to read, simply because there is nothing there in the way of thought or information, we have another large body of writing that offers us most interesting subject matter only to repel us by the constant failure of the author to approximate ease and lucidity in expression.

In America we suffer more than they do in England and France from the naïve style. It is to be found in force in every department of serious prose-writing. One sometimes begins to fear that it may be the typical style in American prose. And if one dwells upon particular authors, it is not that one likes to give offense to individuals, but simply that it is necessary to consider representative cases if one is to understand the wide bearing of the matter, and to give examples if one is to avoid the futility of general statements. Indeed, the persons singled out for notice will naturally be writers of great prominence, and even—if the discussion is to have any point— writers of considerable importance. The main question is how far their addiction to the naïve style affects the degree of their importance. (And are we not getting tired of criticism that consists either of fulsome flattery or of sweeping condemnation? And are we not even ready now to consider how a man writes as well as what he writes about?)

There is Mr. Theodore Dreiser. As a novelist and a writer of autobiography, he attracts us by the solidity of his information upon certain matters of common interest and by the unparalleled honesty and candor with which he goes about to enlighten us. One cannot fail to have a large respect for the author of *A Book about Myself*. In this most unusual autobiography, Mr. Dreiser has given us an illuminating account of newspaper work and the life of newspaper men in the West. He has drawn a picture of himself and his early milieu in Chicago, which is a social document of the highest order; his candor in revealing his own motives of action, the half-humorous detachment with which, in his maturity, he exposes the rawness, the vanity, the flashy vulgarity of himself as a young man, are invaluable in a form of writing in which the characteristic features are disingenuousness, mock-modesty, and the sentimental whitewashing of the writer. He inspires a confidence in the truth of his confessions such as Rousseau fails to inspire. There is a ring of genuineness, a ruthlessness of self-portrayal, not to be found in Huneker's *Steeplejack*, nor even in Mr. Lewisohn's *Up Stream*. The thing reeks with certain American, and for that matter universal human, flavors, that have seldom been more than faintly suggested in print. But, with all these eminent virtues, the book remains a signal and discouraging sample of the naïve style, and the reader is irritated on every page with expressions so blind, with sentences so crudely put together, that however he may be attracted by the man and the matter, he is sure to be repelled by the incoherence of the rhetoric.

It is in our books of travel that the naïve style most infallibly makes its appearance. It is very seldom that we seem able to combine in one person the literary instinct with the curiosity, the wanderlust, the courage, and the enterprise of the traveler who undertakes to bring us detailed information about far places. Mr. Harry A. Franck has given us, I suppose, our most substantial books of information about South America set forth in popular form; his *Working North from Patagonia*, for example, is indispensable to anyone who wishes to travel extensively and intensively in Latin America while staying comfortably by his own fireside. And it would be unfair to criticize him for not having turned out literature when it is so obvious that such an idea never crossed his mind. His sole intention was clearly to give us information historical, topographical, statistical, economic, and social, about South American cities and South American countries. The general quality of the book is well enough suggested by the explanatory legend under the photograph of a street car advertising Scott's Emulsion, "The street cars of Chile are of two stories and have women conductors." That is the sort of thing the reader may learn from Mr. Franck. He will be mightily disappointed if he trusts the promise of the cover, with its picturesque Spanish churches, its glimpse of the matted jungle, and its palmettos rising gracefully over cottage roofs. Mr. Franck is altogether innocent of the picturesque, of the romantic, even of the spirit of adventure; and while he does engage in undertakings which to most of us would seem hazardous and romantic in the extreme, and to which a Stevenson or a Sir Richard Burton would lend some glamor, we get no impression from Mr. Franck but of bodily discomforts suffered in a dreary country. I have no doubt that he has put between his covers five times the information that Mr. H. M. Tomlinson has in any of his books; but Mr. Tomlinson has given us the feel of the Amazon and the jungle, whereas we derive from Mr. Franck nothing more to feed the imagination than the assurance that certain countries are doing well while others are more backward. And the naïve style does nothing to improve the situation.

The case of Mr. Frederick O'Brien is quite a different one. In his various books on the islands of the South Seas he has collected a great number of highly picturesque scenes and incidents which are the stuff of which art is made. I cannot say that he has made very much of this stuff in the way of art, but that is not because he does not recognize its possibilities. It is simply because he does not understand the means by which art is made of such material. There are a half-dozen very fine stories in his single volume, *Atolls of the Sun*. There is, for example, the attempt of Peyral, the French drunkard, to frighten O'Brien into marrying his white daughter, whom he has kept so jealously secluded in their decaying house in the midst of a sordid swamp. One can easily imagine what Conrad might have made of such a situation—his grasp of the psychological values, his working of mystery and suspense, the preparation and the concentration on the most significant scenes. Still better, perhaps, is the narrative of Llewellyn, the half-breed of Tahiti. He tells of the tragic death of his white companion, Willis, along with Taaroa, the woman of Easter Island, whose love he had given up for that of Miss Dorey, daughter of the visiting English savant. We have, to begin with, the setting, the almost depopulated Easter Island, haunted and desolate, mainly inhabited by ancient, gigantic statues of the dead. There is the arrangement of the two sheep-herders, Llewellyn and Willis, by which they borrow for the time of their sojourn the wives of natives—an arrangement equally interesting from the point of view of ethnology and of drama. For upon the arrival of the English scholar and his daughter, jealousy makes its appearance in the breast of Taaroa, a passion heretofore unknown in Easter Island. Follows the festival occasion just before the departure of Willis with the English people, the impassioned dancing of Taaroa, and then the swimming in the ocean. Willis undertakes to drink from the fountain of sweet water which flows into the sea some ten

feet below the surface, and it is necessary for someone to stand upon his shoulders to hold him down
while he drinks. It is Taaroa who volunteers for
this service, with what intentions we are not told.
But the white man and the native woman stay too
long beneath the surface, and when the others dive
and search for them, they are found dead, and locked
together, those two once lovers, caught in the
frightful sponge of kelp and seaweed which has
formed about the issue of the submarine spring.

There is no doubt that Mr. O'Brien has a flair for
the picturesque in scene and story, and that he has
done literature no small service in collecting so
much fine material. If, as some reviewers have suggested, he has drawn considerably on his own invention and his books are not absolutely reliable as
documents . . . . so much the better! In giving us
something to awake our imaginations and to make
his South Seas live for us, he has shown some of
the artistic sense of a Herman Melville, and has
made it less probable that this realm of romance
shall soon go out of the memory of men. He is greatly superior to Mr. Franck in this respect. His books
are at least full of color and of the stuff of drama.
One can imagine these books falling into oblivion,
and then some poet of the future, some story-telling
genius coming upon them, and mining in them for

ore from which to fashion works of art—taking possession of something here and there, and turning it into a thing of beauty and significance.

That is what Mr. O'Brien has not done. He seems never to have rightly envisaged the difference between his book as a collection of miscellaneous information about the South Seas and as a series of pictures and episodes conceived with reference to their aesthetic effect. The stuff is slung together with so little care, with so little consideration for the proper distribution of emphasis, for natural transition and progress, for the bringing out of dramatic values: the sentences overloaded with belated explanations, sentences of narration or description that mistake themselves for sentences of exposition! There is, for the several episodes, no sense of beginning and end, no technique of isolation, of marginal framing and relief. The whole remains in that ill-fated limbo of the journalistic. The stuff is interesting, and we must read, but no chapter takes its place among those shining possessions of the imagination of which Stevenson has bequeathed so many to the world of readers.

I have been speaking of the larger elements of arrangement and structure by which shape and coherence are given to an imaginative conception. As for the lesser details of expression, the case of Mr.

O'Brien is like those of Mr. Dreiser and Mr. Franck, and even perhaps worse, in so far as his subject matter is a little more difficult, his problem of expression more complicated by the finer implications of his dramatic theme. But where the naïve style is concerned it is hardly worth while to try to draw fine distinctions.

The instructed writer is one who understands not merely that words are symbols of ideas, but that they have their connotations and interrelations, and that unless they are put together with care they are likely to get in one another's way, to send the reader off on false scents, and to produce the confusion and distress that notes in music cause us when they are put together without an understanding of the laws of harmony. The instructed writer is like the musician to whom the laws of harmony are so familiar that it has become instinctive in him to observe them, or who at least is aware of the necessity of great deliberation and circumspection in putting the notes together. The naïve writer is one who thinks that all he has to do is to assemble in one sentence or one paragraph the first words that occur to him as symbols of the ideas he wishes to convey, and without any consideration of whether or not they go well together. He has learned, of course, the laws of grammar. But the laws of grammar are very far from standing, in this comparison, for the laws of harmony. Words can be put together in perfect grammatical relationship and make no sense at all, or a sense quite different from that intended by the naïve compounder. It is generally possible for an earnest reader to correct the false impression he first receives and, with a little back-and-forward reference, make out from the context what it is the writer means. But the necessity for such correction makes hard reading, and the writer is likely to have to pay with the ill will, and perhaps with the loss, of his reader. In any case, the latter carries away a kind of indefinable *malaise*, all the stronger as he is himself the better instructed and the more accustomed to an expert handling of words. He feels as if he had been making his way through an uncleared wilderness, painfully circling bowlders and cutting away brush, and swatting insects, and picking himself up after a fall over hidden stumps and roots. And he knows that he has been dealing with a crude and ephemeral piece of work.

For one thing, the naïve writer is unaware of the need for considering the order in which his words follow one another. He writes straight away in the order in which words fall in his language when there is no occasion for making a change. And since he knows quite well himself what it is he means to convey, he has no notion of the difficulty into which he may have plunged his reader by the separation of ideas that belong together or the long delay of some bit of information which it is necessary to have at the start. A brief passage from Mr. O'Brien will illustrate the trouble a naïve writer may cause his readers by simply following the natural order of words in English: subject, predicate, object, adverbial modifiers. He had, he tells us, just returned home after a quarrel with one of the native women which bid fair to be fatal to him.

> I lay down with the Browning beside me, and dreamed that she was testifying against me at the seat of judgment, and that an austere God pointed downward. Exploding Eggs was cooking a rasher of bacon on my improvised stove on the paepae the next morning, when Flag, the mutoi, brought a note, he acting as general manager of the island.

Here we have a sudden passage from night and dreams to morning and the preparation of breakfast. There is no transitional phrase and no paragraph mark to give warning of the change, and we have to wait until a rather long sentence is half through before we can correct our first impression that it was in the dreams of the author on the night of the quarrel that Exploding Eggs was cooking a rasher of bacon. We eventually make that correction, and register one sharp pinprick of irritation at an author who causes us so much trouble. He might just as well have begun his second sentence with the adverbial modifier, "the next morning"; that would have been in accordance with simple English usage, and there would have been nothing sophisticated or Pateresque about it. But it would have been one step removed from the naïve style, and would have cost the writer five seconds of deliberation. His neglect cost the reader at least ten seconds of confusion.

Mr. Franck is if anything still more given to this undeliberate word-order. This is the way he introduces us to the Bolivian gaucho:

As the day was Sunday scores of gauchos *with that half-bashful, laconic, yet self-reliant air common to their class, ranging all the way from half-Indian to pure white in race, with here and there the African features bequeathed by some Brazilian who had wandered over the nearby border,* silently rode up on their shaggy ponies one after another out of the treeless immensity and, throwing the reins of the animal over a fence-post beside many others drowsing in the sun, stalked noiselessly into the dense shade of the acacia and eucalyptus trees about the pulperia, then into the store itself. Most of them were in full regalia of recado, pellones, shapeless felt hat, shaggy whiskers and poncho. [Etc. He continues with the description of them.]

Here is impeccable grammar, the subject modifiers following upon the subject according to the traditional English word-order. But it happens that in this case the subject modifiers, all that I have put in italics, make a passage of forty-one words, and separate the subject from the predicate for an intolerable period during which the reader is held up in gaping discomfort. And it happens, moreover, that all this information belongs naturally to the description of the gauchos which is to follow the account of their arrival, and therefore not in this sentence at all. The least bit of consideration would have led the author to save us all this trouble by the simple expedient of removing the italicized words from their position in the first sentence and giving them a sentence of their own, as follows:

As the day was Sunday scores of gauchos silently rode up on their shaggy ponies one after another out of the treeless immensity and, throwing the reins of the animal over the fence-post beside many others drowsing in the sun, stalked noiselessly into the dense shade of the acacia and eucalyptus trees about the pulpería, then into the store itself. They constitute a class ranging all the way from half-Indian to pure white in race, with here and there the African features bequeathed by some Brazilian who had wandered over the nearby border; and they had that half-bashful, laconic, yet self-reliant air common to their class. Most of them were in full regalia. . . . . [Etc.]

In this case the author fell into the naïve word-order because he did not consider what material belonged in the sentence which he was starting. He took each circumstance as it first came to mind without a moment's consideration of how the several items he had to set forth might best be grouped for effective presentation. And so his sentence turned out amorphous and unwieldy, wanting in that simplicity of thought which is so gratifying to the reader. Oftentimes the naïve word-order results in confusion owing to the doubtful reference of words which have been so placed as to make it questionable to what they are to be applied. Thus in Mr. O'Brien's description of a certain Pacific island, "I hated it at the first view. It was nothing like our South Sea islands, *with black, frowning cliffs* worn into a thousand caves and recesses." The context proves that the phrase, "with black, frowning cliffs, etc.," refers to the hateful island under discussion, but it certainly looks for the moment as if it must refer to "our South Sea islands," to which it is immediately attached.

The difficulty with the naïve writer is that he seems unable to keep together in mind the several items involved in a statement of any complication, so as to realize them in their ensemble, in their relation to one another. The items of the thought he has well in mind of course. At least we need not consider the cases where this is not true. We assume that the writer knows the things he wants to say and the relations they bear to one another in his mind. But he has an imperfect command of the verbal symbols of his ideas and does not take them in at one *coup d'œil*. He does not realize the power they have of taking on, each one, an independent life and force of its own; and how, unless duly watched over, they may begin to quarrel with one another and do a deal of mischief to one another and the general thought. He does not realize the necessity of following through in the later parts of a sentence the train of association started by the words used in the first part. He forgets the precise form and implication of what he has said and goes on to complete the thought with words which do not join on, which imply a different form of phrasing altogether, and which therefore produce the same sense of futility as an unintended dissonance or an unresolved harmony in music. Mr. Dreiser says:

> My favorite pastime, when I was out on an assignment or otherwise busy, was to walk down the streets and view the lives and activities of others, not thinking so much how I might advantage myself and my affairs as how, *for some, the lightning of chance was always striking in* somewhere and disrupting plans, leaving destruction and death in its wake, *for others luck or fortune.*

He means, of course, that for some chance played the destructive part of lightning, for others the benevolent part, let us say, of a fair wind; for some it was bad luck, for others good fortune. What he does say is that for some the baleful lightning of chance leaves death and destruction, for others it leaves good luck. But that makes no sense. And while we do make out at last what he means, we never quite recover from the foolishness of what he says. Or again he says of a certain hospital, "The number of patients doped or beaten or thrown out, and the *number and quality* of operations conducted by incompetent or indifferent surgeons, was known and *shown to be large*." Of course we understand that the quality of operations cannot be shown to be either large or small. Mr. Dreiser has forgotten that the subject of his verb is "quality" as well as "number" of operations. He means to say that the number of operations conducted by incompetent or indifferent surgeons, and consequently of an inferior quality, was shown to be large. He has used the word "quality" where it is obviously superfluous; for what need is there to characterize the quality of operations conducted by incompetent or indifferent surgeons?

Now it is quite true that there is a large class of readers who will be much less bothered by such inept writing than the instructed and fastidious reader of this essay and its carping, finicky author. They are for the most part what we may call "naïve readers," and theirs is a blessed state. They are accustomed to read rapidly and to take in the writer's meaning in a gross, approximate way. They do not ask themselves whether or not the several things he says in a sentence swear at one another. This class of readers makes up a very large part of the reading public. It is to such readers, I fancy, that Mr. Harry Franck addresses himself, and he is no doubt right in not troubling himself overmuch with precision and elegance in his writing. He will "get away" well enough with what he undertakes. Perhaps even Mr. Dreiser and Mr. O'Brien may comfort themselves with a like consideration. But I believe they would be mistaken in doing so. They are aiming higher. They are writing literature, and they would like to be taken seriously. And the naïve reader will never take them seriously, since he has no idea of what is meant by artistic seriousness. He swallows his bait whole, and it makes little difference whether it is minnows, red flannel, or the cunningest of flies. He is no more conscious of the fine effect in writing than of the gross and hit-or-miss. Indeed, he is not at all aware of the fine effect, whereas he is bound, even he, to be vaguely troubled by the roughness of the hit-or-miss. If the author has any fine intentions, let him look not for appreciation to the naïve reader. It is the small body of instructed readers who, in the long run, determine whether a given writer is of great importance, of small importance, or of no importance whatever. It is they who will before very long determine how well Mr. Dreiser and Mr. O'Brien are worth reading.

I am not at all sure what their decision will be. It depends, to begin with, on the importance of this thing we call "style," and whether it counts for 10 per cent in determining the rank of an author, or 50 per cent, or 90 per cent. And on that matter I have not made up my mind. Nor am I prepared to say how surely the naïve style is a token of a naïve mind. It may be that there are authors in whom the naïve style is largely the evidence merely of an inadequate training in expression, and so an accident of their personal history. On the other hand, there are certainly authors in whom the naïve style is the natural accompaniment of a relatively uninstructed mind—or shall we say, a mind which is not given to fine intentions. It is clear that Mr. O'Brien has some valuable artistic endowments. He has a sense of what is picturesque and what is dramatic in literary subject matter. It is more doubtful whether he has the sense of form, that sense which guides the artist in giving dramatic shape to his subject matter. It is possible that he has the artistic temperament without the artistic endowment, and that his unin-

structed style of writing is the mark of an artistical-
ly uninstructed mind.

And so with Mr. Dreiser. He has at least two
very valuable assets of a novelist. He has a large
store of knowledge about human nature, and he has
an honesty in setting forth the truth most unusual
in American literature. He is free to confess that human nature is on the whole gross and treacherous;
and that he has done in several novels and in one
very interesting piece of autobiography. But what
he has to say has been said by many European writers—by Balzac and Zola, by Maupassant and Gorky,
by Arthur Schnitzler and Pio Baroja. They have all
said these things and said them more expertly than
Mr. Dreiser. As one goes on reading Mr. Dreiser one
finds that he has other things to say—things that
imply tenderness and other attractive qualities.
And then one thinks of George Moore and Thomas
Hardy, and again of Gorky and Zola, and one cannot but acknowledge that these things, too, have
been better said by the European writers, with more
grace and finer artistic intention. And one begins to
ask how far Mr. Dreiser's relatively uninstructed
manner of writing is a reflection of something in the
quality of his mind. That is a question one would
like to put to Mr. Mencken, for example. Not that
one expects Mr. Mencken to answer it at this hour

in perfect candor. He has let the world know of the honesty and solidity of Mr. Dreiser; and we must look to some critic who has not passed upon the case to determine whether or not he is an artist of the highest importance . . . . in spite of the naïve style.

OCTOBER, 1925

AUGURIES

AUGURIES

IT may well turn out that the first firm steps of American culture learning to walk the ways of prose may be, not in the road of fiction, but in that of autobiography. Certainly to anyone fresh from the reading of Dostoevsky or Tolstoi, or from that of Flaubert and Zola, our American novels must seem but flimsy confections and hardly meat for men. There is something about the art of fiction, as conceived in Saxon countries, that calls for every sort of faking, padding, vanilla-flavoring, and clove-spicing. We like to think that now, at last, we are telling the truth, though it is our daily experience that the most serious tellers of truth are not to be had in our public libraries; either the books are not on the shelves, or stern women lie to the young men who inquire for them: "We do not have the book you ask for, but we can give you something of Booth Tarkington." We are very "advanced"; our favorite subject is adultery, but we know how to trick it out in a green hat and pass it off for true love sinned against. We have been writing problem novels for decades; and the problem is largely put forward as a substitute for human nature and common sense. Whatever the cause, no one takes very seriously the fictitious inventions of our story-tellers except the literary lady who must provide topics for her dinner-table, or the young Harvard man who has the privilege of a signed review in a New York weekly.

Strange to say, it is when our literary men write about themselves that we can take them seriously. Their material is solid and plentiful. We have no conventions, and few inhibitions, to hamper them in the conduct of this tale of themselves. Their own problems are real enough to bear a straight and eloquent presentation. If they lie about themselves, if they pose and put things in the most attractive light, their very lies and poses are a part of them and make for the essential truth of the record. They are not confined to simple narrative, but have plentiful occasion for reflection, reminiscence, speculation, and are more likely to find themselves writing passages of beauty and charm—*belles pages*, capable of being read a second time, capable of bearing a heavier weight of critical attention than the hastily spun cobwebs of their fiction.

And in their own account, these literary men stand out as men representative of our age of molting and refeathering more unmistakably than the paler creatures of their imagination. We are assuredly a self-conscious age, and particularly we in America are strenuously given to the task of finding ourselves in a world of shifting values, each of which must be questioned long and sharply and taken at the last on trial. America has been seized with a perfect fury of self-criticism since the first well-bred examination by Randolph Bourne. The Philistine in our midst has been staggering under the blows of Mencken and Brooks; the Revolutionary patriot has been shown to be a fallible man with an ax to grind; democracy has been exposed; the American of yesterday has been psychoanalyzed by Mr. Harvey O'Higgins in the persons of two dozen headliners; Mr. Werner has been showing up the fakes and showmen; Mr. Robinson has exposed the dirty roots of our prejudices; Mr. Waldo Frank has interpreted us to our French allies in a spirit equally compounded of explanation, apology, and hopeful prophecy. So massive is the movement against Philistinism, so full the chorus of critics, that one has the impression that the enemy is about to be surrounded and destroyed. It takes a cool bath of history and psychology to remind us that his strength is that of the earth itself, and that nothing short of the fourth dimension is likely to dislodge him from his dominant position.

THE OUTLOOK FOR AMERICAN PROSE

Our literary autobiographies are a product of this movement against the Philistine. And it is this social and aesthetic *tendenz*, which is their common feature and principle of organization, that gives them unity and significance beyond that of the personal record. The tradition goes back rather far, at least as far as *The Education of Henry Adams*. I do not mean that this book was a protest against Philistinism, industrialism, or whatever it is that has us by the throat. Henry Adams was not a protesting kind of man. He was too well bred, too well read, for that. He was too much of a historian, a determinist. He accepted the Dynamo as the genius of our age, and instead of complaining of the Dynamo, he complained of his old-world, old-fashioned education that taught him to understand languages, diplomacy, and the Virgin, but to understand nothing of the Dynamo except its mysterious force and the feast of lights it provided for the St. Louis Exposition. But the note of complaint against his education, that is, his unfitness in the world of machines, has been a fruitful source of suggestion to those who complain of the machines themselves. He continued to live, so far as he acknowledged himself to live at all, in the world of the Virgin, and he started the fashion among American literary men of standing before the cathedral of Chartres as before a symbol and sample of something we have sadly lost out of our dynamic—or rather our passively mechanized—existence.

Henry Adams wrote in a period of suspended animation in American art, before this great effort of the "creative spirit"—odious phrase, which I decline to write except between inverted commas—this great effort to free American letters from its frost of traditional timidity. Mr. John Macy wrote, somewhat later in the same intercalary period, his remarkable essay on *American Literature*, in which he could find no one but Mrs. Wharton and Mr. Dreiser to put with the ten British authors who held their place on his "private shelf of contemporary fiction and drama in the English language"; and he figured the American Spirit as "petitioning the Muses for twelve novelists, ten poets, and eight dramatists, to be delivered at the earliest possible moment." Mr. Macy wrote hopefully enough, and there has been some slight recognition of his modest petition on the part of the American Spirit. Henry Adams wrote with resignation of an America equally ignorant of Dante and Lucretius, equally incapable of giving honor to the Virgin or to Venus. "An American Virgin would never dare command; an American Venus would never dare exist." He does not write in protest, for he does not write in hope. But Mr. Sherwood Anderson, who grew up in a backwoods Ohio in which the handicrafts flourished among carpenters and wheelwrights, can still hope and protest. And the philosophic resignation of Henry Adams becomes in Anderson an energy and an inspiration. In *Many Marriages* the Virgin is startlingly set up as a symbol of some idea quite foreign to the twelfth-century Christian. Venus, though perhaps not Lucretian, is ever present in his stories. And the very words of Henry Adams appear in *A Story-Teller's Story* as slogan of one who would free American fiction from the curse of the machine-made article.

For anyone on the lookout for good prose written by Americans of our time, *The Education of Henry Adams* will naturally be the first book to throw its monumental shadow over his consciousness. But to call this American prose is perhaps to stretch the definition of the term. To him applies more than to any American of our time the words of Matthew Arnold which he applied to the poetry of Tennyson, and which Watts-Dunton applied to Arnold. Watts-Dunton says:

> In one of his own most charming critical essays Arnold contrasts the poetry of Homer, which consists of "natural thoughts in natural words," with the poetry of Tennyson,

which consists of "distilled thoughts in distilled words." To most people the waters of life come with all their natural qualities—sweet or bitter—undistilled. Only the ordinary conditions of civilization, common to all, flavored the waters of life to Shakespeare, to Cervantes, to Burns, to Scott, to Dumas, and those other great creators whose minds were mirrors—broad and clear—for reflecting the rich drama of life around them. To Arnold the waters of life came distilled so carefully that the wonder is that he had any originality left.

Watts-Dunton does, indeed, think that Arnold had plenty of originality left, and it is as clear to us now that *Culture and Anarchy* was the most original book of its day in England as that *The Education of Henry Adams* was the most original book of its day in America. As for the latter, to many of us it was so original, so subtle in conception and progress of the argument, that we had to wrinkle our brows over more than one of its triumphant chapters.

But *Culture and Anarchy* was British in every turn of phrase and every nuance of irony; and the American reader has before his eyes and ears, even to the sideburns and the British drawl, the professor of poetry who came to us to recommend the study of Greek as a specific for our ugliness and aridity. (Another ancestor, by the way, of Van Wyck Brooks and all the rest of our protestants.) Whereas in the manner of Henry Adams it is impossible to catch the accent of the American, certainly for us who pitch our tents beside the Mississippi. The communication is dated from Washington, but it really hails from somewhere in the stars equidistant from London, Rome, Boston, and Mont-Saint-Michel. It is beautiful, it is strong, it is as simple as it could possibly be under the circumstances. It is in the best tradition of English international prose, from Irving to Havelock Ellis. But since Mr. Mencken wrote *The American Language*, we have grown jealous of the word American. We have grown jealous, and proud, and modest; and it is our modesty and our pride together which forbid us to claim Henry Adams as they forbid us to claim George Santayana. Let one but look at the admirable paragraph on the Unitarian clergymen of his Boston youth, a passage calling for nothing in the way of metaphysical subtleties, and one again which suggests the current *tendenz* since it hints the intellectual impotence of the Boston high-brows.

Nothing quieted doubt so completely as the mental calm of the Unitarian clergy. In uniform excellence of life and character, moral and intellectual, the score of Unitarian clergymen about Boston, who controlled society and Harvard College, were never excelled. They proclaimed as their merit that they insisted on no doctrine, but taught, or tried to teach, the means of leading a virtuous, useful, unselfish life, which they held to be sufficient for salvation. . . . . Of all the conditions of his youth which puzzled the grown-up man, this disappearance of religion puzzled him most. The boy went to church twice every Sunday; he was taught to read his Bible, and he learned religious poetry by heart; he believed in a mild deism; he prayed; he went through all the forms; but neither to him nor to his brothers or sisters was religion real. Even the mild discipline of the Unitarian Church was so irksome that they all threw it off at the first possible moment, and never afterwards entered a church. The religious instinct had vanished, and could not be revived, although one made in later life many efforts to recover it. That the most powerful emotion of man, next to the sexual, should disappear, might be a personal defect of his own; but that the most intelligent society, led by the most intelligent clergy, in the most moral conditions he ever knew, should have solved all the problems of the universe so thoroughly as to have quite ceased making itself anxious about past or future, and should have persuaded itself that all the problems which had convulsed human thought from earliest recorded time, were not worth discussing, seemed to him the most curious phenomenon he had to account for in a long life.

That is certainly a most admirable passage, full of intellectual vigor and penetration, and I have often quoted it in my classes by way of making the students understand what it is that Newman meant when he asserted in *The Tamworth Reading Room* that the religion of Protestants tends to be notional or literary rather than real. But then I am infallibly reminded of the strong flavor of Newman in his controversial tracts, a flavor which is more than the emanation of intellectual energy—it is the emanation of intellectual passion, and it runs into aphorism and irony as inevitably as water runs into a depression of the soil.

I have no confidence, then, in philosophers who cannot help being religious, and are Christians by implication. . . . . Logic makes but a sorry rhetoric with the multitude; first shoot round corners, and you may not despair of converting with a syllogism. Tell men to gain notions of a Creator from his works, and, if they were to set about it (which nobody does), they would be jaded and wearied by the labyrinth they were tracing. . . . . Logicians are more set upon concluding rightly, than on right conclusions. . . . . Life is not long enough for a religion of inferences; we shall never have done beginning, if we determine to begin with proof. . . . . Resolve to believe nothing, and you must prove your proofs and analyze your elements, sinking further and further, and finding "in the lowest depth a lower deep," till you come to the broad bosom of scepticism. . . . . Life is for action. If we insist on proofs for everything, we shall never come to action: to act you must assume, and that assumption is faith.

This is Newman, and it is Oxford. One might almost declare that it is Oriel College. It is distilled waters, but not so well distilled but what there remains a strong tincture of sulphur and of iron. There is in it the self-command of a trained writer; but there is not the self-possession of Henry Adams. To make it clearer why one hesitates to characterize Adams as distinctively American, it is worth while to call to mind certain passages in two more recent autobiographies, written by men for whom the

waters of life were not so jealously distilled. The inimitable second chapter of Mr. Kreymborg's *Troubadour* is entitled "Ollie Goes to Church." But it is
really an account of what kept little Ollie and his
mother and father from going to church. Remember
that the elder Kreymborg was the proprietor of a
very modest cigar store in downtown New York.

With respect to the example his parents set by never attend-
ing church themselves, one might have questioned: "Why
were they so lax or lackadaisical?" Had one put that question
to an older Ollie, a being beginning to look back in retrospect,
he would have answered: "It must have been this way. Sunday was the busiest day of the week in the life of my parents.
It was then that most other people were free and more cus-
tomers came in than at any other time. They began coming in
fairly early, and my mother, who was always up first, had to
be sure to sweep the store—scrub it a bit, if necessary—and yet
not confuse the needs of the store with the needs of the household: those *Pfannekuchen*, for example. In the midst of prepara-
tions in the rear, she was often interrupted by the bell out
front—which meant that someone was in a passionate hurry
for some Virgin Leaf or Honest Long Cut, a General Lee or a
General Grant, Sweet Caporals or Lucky Strikes. . . . . If my
mother had an occasion for her religion or faith or whatever it
was she believed in, Sunday was scarcely the day for it. . . . .

"As to what my father was doing meanwhile, this question
is more disconcerting. Most of the time he was helping Mother
in the store, but the rest of the time—well, he liked to read the
Staats Zeitung, and find out if those Lumpengesindel, the Tam-
many Tigers, would carry New York again. Only to resign
politics to politicians and turn to the chess column with:

'Hello—Lasker beat Steinitz—how could that happen—I must play that game over—the store can wait—here, Ollie, come—set up the pieces—Steinitz must be growing old to lose to such a youngster. . . . .'

"You might have seen, even had you eyed him casually, that Father must have been an athlete in his youth. He had gone to the gymnasium in Germany, to the *Turn Verein* over here, and had had his period of strenuous military training. Had you watched his bearing, you would have seen why he had to have his Sunday constitutional—only to Central Park—'I'll be back soon.' . . . . He could hardly be expected to spend the whole of a Sunday indoors—or to devote his hour of freedom to another building—church or no church. If he had time for his religion or faith or whatever it was kept him going, Sunday was frankly not the day for it. Had one put such a question to him, he would have replied, as he replied to all metaphysical queries: *Dummheiten.* Or he would have compromised, in an effort to keep up with the times, by breaking into the German-American *patois* he had started to acquire: *Es ist no use dass mann talken tut.*

"Something kept him going, and something kept her going—though they had lost a good deal so far, were to lose a deal more, and were, finally, to lose each other. For want of a sharper epithet, one has to call it—something. This was never discussed in the household. Few real things were ever discussed. It was not alone that all four—father, mother, Carl, Ollie—were a reticent group. There was so little time for talk —or for talk without interruption. Moreover, each of the males lived his own life. And the woman helped them live it. There is hardly an exact definition or word for such a condition or circumstance. One might call it solitude, aspiration, dreams, individuality, loneliness—and still fall wide of the truth. . . . ."

It would be an endless business pointing out all the features of this writing that mark it as distinctive of Kreymborg as well as of America. As for its Americanism, after the rich and pungent subject matter, there are many small points of expression that one may pick out as having the exact accent, the right smack. "It must have been this way." "But the rest of the time—well, he liked to read the *Staats Zeitung* and find out if. . . . ." There is, above all, perhaps, the disposition to regard as beyond definition "his religion or faith or whatever it was képt him going,'" the "condition or circumstance" of these people's silent cultivation of their vague but powerful ideal. This is a less sensational rendering of what Sandburg renders in "The Sins of Kalamazoo":

> *Hound dogs with bronze paws looking to a long*
> *horizon with a shivering silver angel,*
> *a creeping mystic what-is-it.*

Mr. Sherwood Anderson has been for long our most striking example of a certain mystic and antinomian religiosity that has no roots in the Old Testament nor even in the New Testament as still interpreted by the churches. And there is in *A Story-Teller's Story* a passage in this vein which will bring to the reader airs strongly scented with the rank growths of the Mississippi basin. It is the passage

in which on a moonlit night he reflects on the meaning of Alonzo Berners, the sickly young man whom
he has rescued from the apaches in a Chicago saloon
and brought back to his home in a small Illinois
town—the young man whom everyone loves for the
brotherly good feeling he radiates about him with
his gentle smiling silence, and who reveals to young
Anderson another outlook upon life than that cyn-
icism and hard egoism in which he was earlier in-
doctrinated by Judge Turner.

There was no doubt I was in a magnificent mood and that
I enjoyed it and when I got to the old town I went and stood by
a small brick building that had once been a residence but was
now a cowshed. In a near-by house a child cried and a man and
a woman awoke from sleep and talked for a time in low
hushed voices. Two dogs came and discovered me where I
stood in the silence. As I remained unmoved they did not know
what to make of their discovery. At first they barked and then
they wagged their tails, and then, as I continued to ignore
them, they went away looking offended. "You are not treat-
ing us fairly," they seemed to be saying.

"And they are something like myself," I thought, looking
at the dusty road on which the soft moonlight was falling and
smiling at nothingness.

I had suddenly an odd, and to my own seeming ridiculous
desire to abase myself before something not human and so
stepping into the moonlit road I knelt in the dust. Having no
God, the gods having been taken from me by the life about me,
as a personal God has been taken from all modern men by a
force within that man himself does not understand but that is

called the intellect, I kept smiling at the figure I cut in my own eyes as I knelt in the road and as I had smiled at the figure I had cut in the Chicago saloon when I went with such an outward show of indifference to the rescue of Alonzo Berners.

There was no God in the sky, no God in myself, no conviction in myself that I had the power to believe in a God, and so I merely knelt in the dust in the silence and no words came to my lips.

Did I worship merely the dust under my knees? There was the coincidence as there is always the coincidence. The symbol flashed into my mind. A child cried again in a near-by house and I presume some traditional feeling come down from old tellers of tales took possession of me. My fancy played with the figure of myself in the ridiculous position into which I had got and I thought of the wise men of old times who were reputed to have come to worship at the feet of another crying babe in an obscure place. How grand! The wise men of an older time had followed a star to a cowshed. Was I becoming wise? Smiling at myself and with also a kind of contempt for myself and my own sentimentality I half decided I would try to devote myself to something, give my life a purpose. "Why not to another effort at the rediscovery of man by man?" I thought rather grandly, getting up and beating the dust off my knees, the while I continued the trick I had learned of pointing the laughing finger of scorn at myself. I laughed at myself but all the time kept thinking of the occasional flashes of laughter that came from the drawn lips of Alonzo Berners. Why was his laughter freer and more filled with joy than my own?

This is hardly the spirit in which young Wordsworth discovered, after a wakeful night, that he was to be a "dedicated spirit." Sherwood Anderson is certainly self-conscious; he is certainly, as we Americans have the habit of saying, sophisticated. He has learned the trick of pointing the laughing finger of scorn at himself. And it may have been from Henry Adams, among others, that he learned this trick. But for the rest the two men bristle with differences. And it is not most of all the images which create the scene for the imagination—the cowshed, the crying child, the dusty road, the moonlight—that make the difference. Nor is it, most of all, the quality of the sentiment. It is the looseness of the weave, the prominence of the pattern, and the breadth of the rhythm. "I went and stood." "Dogs came and discovered me. . . . ." That, and the punctuation, will do for the looseness of the weave. . . . . Henry Adams is broadcloth, and his is a seamless raiment.

No, decidedly. Henry Adams is a quarry for Americans to dig in. He is a liberal education for us. He is a monument for Americans to point to with pride. But in the movement anticipated by Mr. Macy, in which provincialism was to be avoided by writers smacking of the soil, Henry Adams does not "belong." He is an asset, but hardly an augury.

"STEEPLEJACK"

Nor can I feel that the author of *Steeplejack* "belongs." Certainly Huneker is in the movement of ideas which have loosed the American tongue. He has dared much in his initiations into the literature of the world. He has spread his table with exotic dishes which make the Philistine foam at the mouth. He has filled the columns of newspapers with matters which are the amazement of editors. But his *Steeplejack* rings in my ear with a falsetto note. It is so jolly and bumptious, it has so much of the brogue of an Irishman playing the man of the world, it is so facile and journalistic! It is certainly a valuable document in the history of American literature. But I do not feel certain that it quite qualifies either as American or as literature.

"UP STREAM"

With regard to *Up Stream*, I am of a more divided mind. It is of course an important book, but I do not feel sure as to the degree of its importance. It is a very serious arraignment of race prejudice and of Puritanism, of an indubitable sincerity and power. The picture of the author's parents isolated and spiritually obstructed by their double handicap of German and Jew is both touching and beautiful in its spirit, as is his account of his own enthusiastic espousal of Saxon poetry and culture. And it may well be that I put an extravagant valuation on manner in writing as opposed to matter. I have failed to find in this volume passages that seem to me capable of being put alongside of passages from the finest prose-writers—Rémy de Gourmont, say, or Bernard Shaw.

There is better writing, if I am not mistaken, in his more recent volume of criticism, *The Creative Life*. There is, for example, the admirable passage in which he tells how he has fallen between the two stools of the academic and the journalistic, and has consequently failed to please either his university colleagues or his free-lance rivals in New York. "I knew from the beginning that I would please no one." And there are occasional sayings of aphoristic fineness reminding one of his master, Goethe: "A people that crushes the creative will has only an Egyptian future and will leave as its chief monument a tomb reared by a slave."

In *Up Stream* it is not his occasional betrayal that he was not born to the English idiom that bothers me. I am afraid we shall have to reconcile ourselves to the occasional misfit of a preposition so long as we have the privilege of welcoming writers whose parents spoke a foreign language. They bring us matters so much more important than precision in the use of English prepositions. And I do not suppose I should hold it against Mr. Lewisohn that he shows no sense of humor. Depth and intensity of feeling are of course more important than the ability to treat a serious matter lightly. And yet somehow I cannot persuade myself that the pages of Mr. Lewisohn on prohibition and its allies make as good reading as Mr. Mencken's. I admire the spirit of humanity in which they are written; I admire the intensity of feeling, and warm to the man who has such warmth himself. But I cannot help marking the phrases of railing emphasis, as I shall italicize them in the passage I quote, and I feel that the phrases, if not the feelings they express, betray a lack of some of the elements of good sense. Of prohibition he says:

Each time the question came up I found my Anglo-American friends succumbing a little more and a little less willing to protest against the *raucous propaganda*. It became in the end almost "bad form." In the first place, twenty-one states were already dry—even Michigan. So the *terrible fatalism* of democracy, inherent in its worship of majority opinion and its fundamental rejection of qualitative distinctions, was making itself felt more and more. If a disease spreads, expose yourself to it. Why should you want something better than others? I found my acquaintance almost *so sodden in their folly*. Furthermore—it was a question of morals and they had an *unconquerable hesitation toward taking a negative attitude* [here the overheated pen slips and blots the page with obscurity] on a question of morals. Even those who were not at all fanatical and themselves drank were willing to let things take *their evil course:* "It does nobody any good; it does some people harm; I mustn't be selfish. . . . ." They looked at me with estranged eyes when

I said: "I'd be willing to take an oath never to touch fermented liquor again if only I could save our people from *the infamy of prohibition.*"

But most of my friends were, in some strange way, hypnotized by the *fevered fanatics* of the Anti-Saloon League and the Evangelical Churches. No one seemed to understand the character of *these poor creatures.* They can no longer burn witches or whip Quakers. They have somehow lost their grip on the devil of old. So they have made the substance known as ethyl alcohol into an overshadowing myth—the evil thing in the world that must be fought and trodden underfoot and exorcised by Christian men. Since they cannot quite in this age say that I am an unbelieving dog, they say—with sternly pitying and averted faces—that I shall die a drunkard. It is, of course, because in their *savage and yet festering souls* they have never caught a glimpse of the meaning of humane culture—choice, self-direction, a beautiful use of all things. These poor slaves of drink must either howl against it or reel in the barrooms. One knows the type: thin-lipped, embittered by the poisons that unnatural repression breeds, with a curious flatness about the temples, with often, among the older men, a wiry, belligerent beard. You have seen them with their shallow-bosomed, ill-favored wives—stern advocates of virtue—walking on Sunday self-consciously to church. The wine they have never tasted, the white beauty they have never seen, the freedom of art they have never known—all their unconscious hungers have turned to gall and wormwood in their crippled souls.

Here is a fine indignation. Here are even fine strokes; but they are fine in proportion as the author turns his sarcasm in the direction of ironic description rather than in that of invective and epithet. One is tempted to say of such writing, "There is something Prussian about this, something over-blunt and rigid, something military. There are moments when Mr. Lewisohn is in danger of classifying himself with the fanatics whom he opposes." Mr. Lewisohn has given perhaps in *The Creative Life* the clue to his comparative failure to make literature. He says that, as time goes on, he cares less and less for art in its abstract forms and more and more for life. And when he speaks of life, he means, so far as the artist is concerned, propaganda, or—less invidiously—the turning of art to the service of human causes. He is confronted with a choice between being an aesthete and a pamphleteer, and he chooses the latter. "A pamphleteer, by all means. Even a pamphleteer needn't write ill. Lessing was one, Swift another."

Those are noble models, but dangerous to cite. For it is doubtful whether either one was primarily a pamphleteer; and in any case they were writers who did not allow their devotion to a cause to interfere with the purity of their writing. Swift wrote his *Modest Proposal* out of an indignation as well grounded as Mr. Lewisohn's, but he did not allow a pebble of ill-directed sarcasm to trouble the surface of his terrible irony. And he produced a work of art the like of which we have never conceived in cause-ridden America. Voltaire was a pamphleteer and an obstinate and devoted defender of special causes that hung from the general cause of liberty and justice and freedom of thought. He snatched men from the maw of the Bastille. But where can you find in *Candide* or *Zadig* an instant's departure from the tone set for these Martian surveys of terrene affairs? Anatole France has doubtless served as well as anyone of his day the cause that Mr. Lewisohn proposes: "humane culture—choice, self-direction, a beautiful use of all things." But he has not found it incompatible with the preservation of his artistic self-command. In speaking in *Up Stream* of the censorship of literary art, and with particular reference to the suppression of Mr. Dreiser's novel, *The Genius*, Mr. Lewisohn says, "I am not able, as some of my liberal New York friends are, to take a humorous view of this situation." That is really his loss. The American endowment which he most needs is our humor. Our humor is not necessarily a confession of supineness, as Mr. Lewisohn intimates in regard to the humorous attitude of his New York friends. It is often a philosophical recognition of facts of rather large bearing: the fact that no one of us is going to determine whether the country shall be wet or dry; the fact that the cause of justice and liberty is not going to be won or lost in one generation or in a hundred generations; the fact that few causes are so important as the cultivation of one's own garden. And more than that, our humor —or shall we say, less pertly, humor in general?— is often a better weapon than indignant sarcasm for the forwarding of whatever cause. It is a great force in human life, a sapper and miner, an instrument of great power to "pry loose old walls," to "lift and loosen old foundations."

I am reminded of the gentle and persistent play of whimsical humor throughout Mr. Kreymborg's record in *Troubadour*. Mr. Kreymborg is as stout a fighter as Mr. Lewisohn, and has suffered as long and bravely the east wind of philistine neglect and scorn. Innumerable are the forces he has found arrayed against his simple wish to be a poet and to see good poetry prevail. The stupid editors who invariably returned his manuscripts, and who insisted on printing the vile stuff which would please their readers; their readers, the same choosers of the mechanical and standardized who preferred the cheap products of the tobacco syndicate to the real Havana segars made by the hands of his father; the Poetry Society; the leaders of schools of poetry of which he did not approve and who did not approve of him; the divorce laws of New York State; the system of public education in which he proved a failure; and the industrial system in which he found it so hard, with the best of wills, to earn his bread and butter. How often he must have set his teeth in hatred of a world so opposed to all his wishes and needs! And yet there is not a word of hatred and indignation, nor a word of despair, in the whole book, though he is still struggling as the uncompromising must struggle in a world of accommodation and adjustment. It is clear enough what he thinks of it all, and that he has kept untainted for more than forty years the simple idealism of his foreign parents. But he early acquired a magic faculty for detachment whereby he may survey himself and the world opposing him from a certain distance and with a mildly humorous comprehension of himself and it. What views he gives of himself going about in pursuit of some editorial dream—absent-minded, nearsighted, with his shoes in such a state, the tobacco and coffee stains on his clothes, forever repairing the knot in the black ribbon that attached his pince-nez to his top vest-button, and frantically trying to explain to his latest victim the idea of this new publication! How sympathetically he presents the spiritual situation as it affected him and the other man involved!

One might have mistaken him for a panhandler. But there was something so immediately sensitive in the way he acted if one betrayed such a thought that one had to employ the most subtle subterfuge to get him to forget the incident. And one had to be careful not to express anything symptomatic of pity or sympathy. He wanted to interest a person, if it was possible to interest him, in the thing which haunted and drove him about. That was all. . . . .

Mr. Kreymborg has never owned a motor car, and with humorous pathos he makes note of the first one he ever rode in; but he registers no note of indignation against the banker who took him into his car, or against Wall Street or the economic system that apportions motor cars to some while others go on foot with leaky soles. One of his loveliest chapters is that entitled "The Latest Improvements." It has in it the stuff of heartbreak; for it is in this chapter that the family moved to Brooklyn under the impulse of a real estate boom, that brother Carl was married, that the handmade cigars were driven off the market by the United Cigars syndicate, and that Ollie's father put off any further venture in business so that he might look after the mother who was dying of cancer—a disease from which she had long suffered in silence in order not to worry the husband and the son who would be married. Alfred Kreymborg does not fail to render the atmosphere of a real estate boom, nor the swoop across the land of the specters of machine-production and standardization and economic "optimism." But these are things he can well understand as expressions of fundamental human nature; and he renders them in their own terms, including their very view of himself and his father. "Only a reactionary like Ollie's father or a whippersnapper like Ollie was blind to the trend of the times. What did the old fogy come over here for, why didn't he stay where he belongs, the flying Dutchman? He and his measly, ten-cent, home-made Havana weeds!"

Mr. Kreymborg, too, has his ideas on the censorship, and has had occasion to describe the dealings of the Society for the Prevention of Vice with one of his own books. But he has managed to tell the story most amusingly, and without a curse on either Mr. Sumner his prosecutor, or his unwelcome defender, Mr. Frank Harris, or even upon the publisher who exploited the scandal and used it for his own sole benefit. In regard to Guido Bruno, he contents himself with remarking drily, "The publisher must have earned quite a tidy sum, since the author never received a cent."

Yes, I must confess to a preference for the right manner, and I love Mr. Kreymborg's finesse better than the righteous indignation of Mr. Lewisohn. But for all that one cannot but regard *Up Stream* as no mean augury for the future of American prose.

"A BOOK ABOUT MYSELF"

It is in a view of *A Book about Myself* that the question of manner versus matter becomes most acute, and for me insoluble. It is one of the most fascinating books I have ever read, so far as matter is concerned. For Mr. Dreiser has in supreme degree the virtue of candor in regarding himself. And he is evidently one of the few men living and writing who look upon life, as I believe all men should look upon it who have any pride of intellect, with fierce and unshrinking regard for the truth. That is the greatest gratification that life can bring to a creature of our genus, unless it be the double prize of seeing and showing the truth. I am not presuming to judge whether Mr. Dreiser is well equipped for determining the truth; but there can be no mistaking the sincerity with which he sets about to do so. And he is in a better position for telling us the truth about himself than about the people of his fictions. Moreover, the man revealed in this confession is a man admirable for other qualities than intellectual passion and energy and the zest of life. He is obviously a lovable man; and there is one unobtrusive passage of domestic feeling for which alone, if I were St. Peter, I would admit him at my jealously guarded gate. It is his account of the scene when he returns to Chicago after a considerable absence and goes to see his broken old father. His father was a Catholic who set immense store by the regular performance of religious duties, but the son had already ceased to be a practicer or believer. And now the old man wishes assurance that he is keeping up his religious duties. And the son, for all his pride of intellect, without hesitation utters the necessary lie:

"Yes, yes," I interrupted, making up my mind to give him peace on this score if I never did another thing in this world, "I always go right along, once every month or six weeks." He was so utterly done for, as he knew [says the son in a tender note of explanation], and dependent on the courtesy of his children and life.

There is no doubt that the man is one to be loved and admired. And yet, reading the book with a strong prepossession in favor of its author, I cannot find a page in the whole book which is beautiful, not a page which can be rejoiced in as a product of literary craft. I have spoken far too often already of the rhetoric of this man. And of that I shall say no word here. I shall confine myself to the question of tone, of taste, and that in the touching of one crucial subject—the subject of sex. And first I shall assemble a half-dozen passages out of a larger number in which he refers to women and his dealings with them, so that we may have a sufficient body of matter upon which to exercise the puzzled mind. I will lump them all together, and leave until later any explanation of context which may be necessary.

I was more of a personage for having had it once more proved to me that I was not unattractive to girls. . . . .

I had hung up my coat and hat with a flourish and had stood about for a while examining everything, with the purpose of estimating it and her. . . . .

I fancy she thought that if she yielded to me physically and found herself with child my sympathy would cause me to marry her. [Here the author pictures the exact circumstances of the young man's trial, and concludes:] I did not think that I ought to do that thing, then. . . . .

What an odd beginning, I often thought to myself. Scandalous, perhaps, in one so young: three girls in as many years, two of them deeply and seriously wounded by me. . . . .

My body was blazing with sex, as well as with a desire for material and social supremacy—to have wealth, to be in society—and yet I was too cowardly to make my way with women readily; rather they made their way with me. . . . .

It does not matter now but as I look back on it there seems to have been more of pure, exalted or frenetic romance in this thing (at first, and even a year or so afterward), than in any mating experience of which I have any recollection, with the possible exception of Alice.

As soon as I try to put into words the impression such passages make upon my aesthetic sensorium, I find two voices speaking in my mind, in impatient and irritable debate.

FIRST VOICE: "I can't help feeling that this is pretty crude."

SECOND VOICE: "What do you mean, crude?

Doesn't the man say in all simplicity what he wants to say? I suppose you are bothered by his 'body blazing with sex.'"

FIRST VOICE: "No, that doesn't bother me. It is a little startling at first, but it is certainly a telling metaphor. He makes me see a young man as an electric battery, charged with power ready to be directed into action useful or destructive, and dangerous to touch for anyone who does not understand the ways of that electric fluid."

SECOND VOICE: "Well, then, I suppose you object to the cynical deliberation of the young fellow estimating the girl and her surroundings, as if he were a merchant come to cheapen goods."

FIRST VOICE: "No, not exactly. Of course, I don't like the idea. But, to tell the truth, we are all merchants in life, however we may disguise the circumstance. The characters in Henry James are always estimating one another and their surroundings. Isabel Archer falls in love with Gilbert Osmond for his Florentine villa, and Lambert Strether gives his shameless attention to every detail of the Parisian salon of Madame de Vionnet. Heaven knows James is not crude, nor has he ever been accused of being materialistic. No, we have here an excellent picture of a fresh young fellow frankly taking in a situation of prime importance to him."

SECOND VOICE: "Well, then, you object to his conceit in saying that he was not unattractive to girls."

FIRST VOICE: "No, that is very good. That is the mature author picturing the conceit of the young man he had been ages ago. And it isn't exactly conceit, either; there is too much intelligence involved. It is sound psychology. Who is not more of a personage for realizing that he has produced a good effect on others?"

SECOND VOICE: "Is it then his boast that he has had three girls in as many years, and two of them deeply and seriously wounded by him?"

FIRST VOICE: "Oh no, I don't call it a boast any more than you do. Of course his vanity is involved, but his conscience is also touched; he is really troubled at having aroused affections which he cannot meet. There *is* something about the expression 'deeply and seriously wounded by me'—something bald, something naïve. But I can't say what it is, and I'll let that pass."

SECOND VOICE: "Well, then, what is it you won't let pass?"

FIRST VOICE: "That way of talking about his mating experiences, and the implication of his having had such a multiplicity of mating experiences that he may have lost all recollection of some of them, and the way he has of trying to weigh them in a balance to determine which one had the greatest specific gravity (he is talking of his love for the woman he married). It makes me think of dogs and cats. I cannot imagine a man as serious and conscientious as he forgetting any experience he has ever had of this kind, though God knows a man sniffs at a great number of women in a lifetime. But what about the sentiment connected with these things? What about the compassionate view of 'wounded' women, and the shame one feels over cheap and abortive essays? Are they not enough to keep alive some memory of the thing? George Moore is, by his own account, a man without conscience in these matters, but his aesthetic sense is a strong preservative and embalmer of his dead loves."

SECOND VOICE: "Ah, there you betray yourself. You prefer a sentimental aesthete to a teller of truths. You prefer the musk of Paris to the breath of Lake Michigan. You have yourself praised in Dreiser his fierce and unshrinking regard for the truth, and now on the first occasion you blame him for not wrapping up the truth in the pink and saffron veils of romance. This man is writing in an age of science; he has read Darwin; and he has the courage to view his own experience in terms of biology."

FIRST VOICE: "Cannot one imply the biology without denying the humanity? Cannot one use finesse and yet make himself understood? Must one talk of one's most sacred affection as 'frenetic romance'? Was not the sentiment as actual in the flower as in the roots?"

SECOND VOICE: "The author is describing one of nature's traps. And he is also going on to describe the disastrous effect of social convention which prevented the consummation of this love in the moment of its fragrant opening, and put it off until 'the first flare of love had thinned down to the pale flame of duty.'"

FIRST VOICE: "That is an effective figure, but there is no figure and no touch of art in 'pure, exalted or frenetic romance.' Nor is there any touch of art in that sentence, 'If she yielded to me physically and found herself with child my sympathy would cause me to marry her.'"

SECOND VOICE: "Doesn't he say what he means?"

FIRST VOICE: "He says what he means, but he says it baldly, and he dots his *i*'s with a vengeance. He doesn't need the word 'physically.' We know how women find themselves with child. He doesn't need to write like a treatise on sociology. Is there no other way to make clear what he means? He talks like a Baptist minister."

[231]

SECOND VOICE: "You would rather have him talk like a female novelist mincing over maternity."

FIRST VOICE: "No, I would not have him talk like a female novelist. I would have him talk like a man of the world. I would have him say things like a well-bred and sensible woman. I would have him take his time and consult a dictionary of synonyms."

SECOND VOICE: "What would you say yourself? What do you suggest as a substitute?"

FIRST VOICE: "Oh, I haven't time to do his job for him. It would be necessary to recast the whole thing, to approach the subject with some kind of indirection. These are not things that one blurts out to the first comer. Imagine George Moore saying, 'I did not think that I ought to do that thing, then.' "

SECOND VOICE: "No, he wouldn't say it, for he wouldn't have the scruples of our American realist."

FIRST VOICE: "I mean, if he did have the scruples. Wouldn't he find some way less clumsy, less blunt, and at the same time just as straight?"

SECOND VOICE: "He would find some way less blunt, maybe, but even straighter and more precise. You are really objecting to the delicacy of the young man. For that is just how he would have expressed himself to some friend upon the subject.

Perhaps it is naïve; but there is a touch of conscience there, and a biblical simplicity. 'I did not think that I ought to do that thing.' The only real awkwardness is in the subjoined adverb 'then.' It is rather tacked on. But it is a succinct intimation to the reader that Mr. Dreiser is not so sure now that he was right at the time."

FIRST VOICE: "He is too damned succinct, and too damned crude."

SECOND VOICE: "You are afraid of directness, and afraid of a method which renders the precise accent of the moment and the experience. You don't like Dreiser's tone because he has identified himself completely with the young man whom he is describing, crudenesses and all. You fail to see that this is a stroke of dramatic genius."

And so the apologist has the last word. And the critic is silenced. But still in his heart he shakes his head over the matter. How do I know this is a stroke of genius? It has many of the marks of artistic fumbling. Here is a workman all thumbs.

"TROUBADOUR"

It is not to make invidious comparisons that I take up Mr. Kreymborg's autobiography immediately after that of Mr. Dreiser, or that with Mr. Kreymborg too I find my most crucial examples of his quality in his account of his dealings with women. It is simply that I have at last arrived at a book of which I can speak with unqualified enthusiasm and that, in general, as Meredith long ago noted, in the case of Sir Willoughby Patterne, it is in men's dealings with women that their distinctive quality is most infallibly revealed. And I do not mean to imply that the facts in Mr. Kreymborg's case are to be preferred to the facts in Mr. Dreiser's as subject matter for literary treatment. It may even be that the facts presented by Mr. Dreiser are more typical of American life in general, or even more typical of human nature, and I do not question their importance for literature and for social philosophy. But it so happens that, as the facts presented by Mr. Kreymborg, true as they are, and sad too, are infinitely more attractive, so the manner of presentation is infinitely more expert. The history is one in which all parties concerned, and there are five of them, happen to have exhibited a spiritual grace which is not beyond the scope of humanity, however exceptional it may seem; and to the development of such a theme Mr. Kreymborg has brought a literary grace for which I do not know where to find parallels, above all in American letters.

Throughout the entire narrative one finds it impossible to distinguish sharply between matter and manner. The Odyssey of Mr. Kreymborg is so full of surprises and bizarre circumstances, it is so full of strange combinations and ironic juxtapositions, that one at times inclines to name him bluntly Münchausen as he once names himself in a chapter heading. But that is not fair; he does not really call himself a liar, but acknowledges that the adventures in which he has figured are as incredible as those of the redoubtable baron, and seems to breathe the hope that for all that he may be believed. Perhaps in the character of such a man there is some force which insensibly shapes his life into patterns more interesting than those of other people, as D'Artagnan is sure to be involved with queens and cavaliers in an adventure having for its prizes diamond necklaces and high reputations. There is a suggestion in this poet's career of Perceval, the guileless fool, who by his very folly is privileged to find the Holy Grail. More than once he returns to the German proverb which had been applied to him as a boy by his father, *Noch so alt und doch so dumm.* His *Dummheit,* which is simply unworldliness and singleness of purpose, brings him so often to the Isles of Sirens or into the house of Circe. Perhaps the most amusing adventure in the whole book is that in which the utterly unpolitical poet comes to write, in satirical vein, the keynote speech for a great political convention. His speech is taken seriously and actually delivered to applauding multitudes; and on the very day of his vicarious and anonymous fame in St. Louis, the poet in person is delivering in Chicago an address on the subject nearest to his heart—on "Poetry'"—delivering it to an audience of sixteen people, of whom three are grinning reporters. Is it the circumstance that is most remarkable or the art of the writer who sees its points?

His genius is felt both in the broader aspect of the general conception of episode and epopee and in the narrower phase of the *mot juste*. He has long been a distinguished member of that small group of American poets who are most delicately and acutely sensitive to the values of words, not merely for thought, but for accent and image: Frost, Sandburg, Wallace Stevens, Elinor Wylie, H.D. And among these he has a special kinship with Sandburg and H.D., poets with such an uncanny faculty for reducing the number of words to the barest minimum necessary to carry the poetic intention, and then for arranging these few expressive words in patterns involving a cunning repetition by which they grow in significance and force as musical themes grow and grow in their development. It is not a mere coincidence that *Chicago Poems*, *Sea Garden*, and *Mushrooms* all date from the identical year 1916; and one notes a par-

ticular kinship between the method of Mr. Kreym-
borg and that of Sandburg in such poems as "Clark
Street Bridge," "Sea Slant," and "Without the
Cane and the Derby."

One of the problems in this way of using words
is the problem of number. The theme must be repeated just often enough and not too often. And
there is no meter and no stanzaic norm to determine
the matter. It is an affair of mathematics, like the
number of bars in a piece of music. But it is a mathematics that resides in the ear. It is only the infallible ear that can tell Sandburg how many times the
pendulum should swing in "Without the Cane and
the Derby":

Once more the motions of strangling . . . . then . . . .
nothing at all . . . . nothing at all . . . . no more knocking
. . . . no knocking at all . . . . no knocking at all . . . . in
the time of the human heartbeat.

Or H.D. in "Sea Gods":

For you will come,
you will come,
you will answer our taut hearts,
you will break the lie of men's thoughts,
and cherish and shelter us.

Or Kreymborg in "Vista":

The snow,
ah yes, ah yes indeed,
is white and beautiful, white and beautiful,

[237]

verily beautiful—
from my window.
The sea,
ah yes, ah yes indeed,
is green and alluring, green and alluring,
verily alluring—
from the shore.
Love,
ah yes, ah yes, ah yes indeed,
verily yes, ah yes indeed!

In all these examples the repetition is no more remarkable than the variation; and one of the most engaging forms taken by this playful treatment of words is that in which the repeated word or phrase occurs, not in identical or parallel construction, but in an altered syntactical relation. An example of this mental process operating with fine emotional effect is one of the lines of Fiammetta in Landor's account of Boccaccio's dream. She is speaking of the Lethean water which she and her lover must drink from her crystal vase before they may win oblivion of their carnal love. Boccaccio, in an impulsive embrace, has spilled the water. "I must go down to the brook," said she, "and *fill it again as it was filled before.*" There is a tendency very strong in both Frost and Robinson—in Frost an accompaniment of his whimsey—which, if we could get to the bottom of the matter, would tell us something very intimate about their mental and imaginative quality. It is seen in these lines from "An Old Man's Winter Night," which Mr. Frost himself regards, and not without reason, as the rarest poem in *Mountain Interval*. The out of doors, we have read, is looking darkly in on the old man through the crystals on the window pane:

> *What kept his eyes from giving back the gaze*
> *Was the lamp tilted near them in his hand.*
> *What kept him from remembering what it was*
> *That brought him to that creaking room was age.*

Some of the most effective examples of the same rhetorical spirit in Mr. Robinson are to be found in "Eros Turannos," heightened here by the rhyme as it was heightened in Frost by the blank-verse meter, as in the first stanza:

> *She fears him, and will always ask*
>   *What fated her to choose him;*
> *She meets in his engaging mask*
>   *All reasons to refuse him;*
> *But what she meets and what she fears*
> *Are less than are the downward years,*
> *Drawn slowly to the foamless weirs*
>   *Of age, were she to lose him.*

Or more briefly, in "The Poor Relation," the giant harp of the city blending in its continuous hum

> *The coming of what never comes*
> *With what has past and had an ending.*

Mr. Frost makes his fanciful countryman say in "The Mountain," of the supposed miraculous spring:

> *I don't suppose the water's changed at all.*
> *You and I know enough to know it's warm*
> *Compared with cold, and cold compared with warm.*
> *But all the fun's in how you say a thing.*

This, while it has always been recognized as a principle most true for poetry, does suggest that the thing we have under observation partakes of something other than the pure spirit of lyrical feeling. It is more akin to the spirit of a child playing with words to see what can be done with them, or with that of the metaphysician playing with ideas. For the child playing with words, there is something animated and magical about these tricky entities, and he is inclined more than half to let them play their own game, like a hand writing on a ouija board. Mr. Kreymborg has carried this game to greater lengths than any of his American contemporaries, as in his delicious Dadaist "Hen Being," or in his plays, where the words take on a wilful animation almost greater than that of the puppet-like characters. But he has also played it with discretion in poems grave and philosophical as "Dirge" in *Less Lonely:*

AUGURIES

Death alone
takes what is left
without protest, criticism
or a demand for more
than one can give
who can give
no more than was given.

This little trick of contemporary poetry—and it is not confined to American poets—may come in time to be recognized as a sort of equivalent of the "wit" which was such a feature of Pope and Dryden, taking in them so largely the form of an antithesis conformable to the genius of the heroic couplet. It goes, like the Augustan wit, with extreme fastidiousness and the aristocratic concern for style. It goes, like that, with a distinctly philosophical bent. Only it has, as that does not often have, the freshness and naïveté of the child's feeling for words —you will find it in Hilda Conkling, too; it is less purely an intellectual formulation of experience; and it naturally accompanies the sharply imaginative effect of "An Old Man's Winter Night," the tense emotion of "Eros Turannos," or the fanciful sentiment, the emotional overtones, the liveliness of imagery of Kreymborg, as in his "Lima Beans" or "In a Dream."

It is, then, with such a training and background that Mr. Kreymborg comes to the writing of prose.

But I would not have the reader suppose that there is much exhibition in *Troubadour* of this peculiar rhetoric. I expect that Kreymborg will go on to write prose of a more purely imaginative cast, in which he will doubtless make use of many of the devices he has tried out in verse. But here he is engaged in the simple task of telling the story of his life, a story bristling with information precise and objective. And his style is always sufficiently simple and business-like. There is but one passage in which he gives liberal rein to his love of shuffling words like colors. It is in his charming Prelude, where he tells us of the young poets so lonely in their monachal attics, and how they come to one another on the rare occasions when, instead of the eternal anonymous rejection slips from the magazines, some editor has condescended to write in person and explain the return of a manuscript. He is at the point where such a favored young man has come in to see him.

As he drew nearer, trying to put on a casual air, and you waited for him to unfold the famous document, a host of slender slips of printed paper, oblong parallelograms, pink, blue, gray, green, brown, began a slow, mocking dance in your brain, while you sat in a corner and watched them, dully wondering how many more would join the dance, how many more would the postman bring, how many more would you walk to the bottom of four flights of stairs to remove from your black tin box in the vestibule and climb to the top of four flights of stairs to slit open and release, along with the rejected manuscript, the sheets you had typed so neatly, folded so neatly, sent so neatly, the white thing you had spent so many hours on, days on, weeks on, so much energy, blood, hope, doubt, despair, trying to make it speak, to fill it with you, cajoling it, imploring it, revising it, only to have it return, speechless, helpless, inanimate, folded where you had folded it, with the identical creases, and no sign to betray the thing had been touched at all, not even a smudge or a thumb print to prove the thing had ever left you, no clue but another dancer, quite like the last, pink, blue, gray, green. . . . .

Mr. Kreymborg has not, in general, a mannered or eccentric style in prose, and I am not prepared to point out the features by which he might be spotted in anonymous passages such as college students must identify. The flavor is constant. But only occasionally a page is salted with some locution comparable with those we find so characteristic of his poetry. He speaks of the discretion of his hostess at Silvermine while he and Christine are falling in love during their rehearsals. But she must have known what was going on. "And what that courteous critic didn't know might have been imparted by a tennis court where Christine and Krimmie volleyed at each other. Or certain paths in certain woods, and stumps of fallen trees." There were on each side engagements which stood in the way of their growing love, and they tried hard to be loyal to their previous engagements. But there came a time in the fall when New England beckoned bewitchingly to the lovers. "Every element in the sky, air and earth conspired against loyalties. Once more a full moon, not entirely unrelated to the moon of a summer night, innocently supplied the coup de grâce. And the woods gave the wanderers the solitude they required for saying what it was they had to say."

The style is uniformly graceful, delicately tinted, and saturated, if one may speak so, with humorous detachment. And if I dwell on the story of his heart, it is because there more than anywhere else the graceful, delicate, and humorous style is the most perfect rendering of the spirit of the thing. It may be that Mr. Kreymborg has somewhat arranged this story; it seems incredible that events should have fallen out so prettily as they did. But then we can only say that his arrangement is all that it should be, and that such a pattern of human relations is the most creditable to human nature next to the highly difficult pattern of one-love-and-happy-ever-after. There is first the long affectionate camaraderie of Krimmie and Tommy—Tommy, the rich girl somewhat older than Krimmie who cannot marry a threadbare poet or even make known his existence to a father with more exalted ideas. The strain is a hard one, and there comes a time when depression falls upon them and the shadow of temperamental difference. And this depression does not divide them; for, comrade-like, they share it. That is indeed the beautiful note of all these episodes; the thing that divides the loves of man and woman seals them closer in friendship and humanity. Then comes the sojourn at Silvermine and the revelation of budding April in Christine. Krimmie and Christine struggle against disloyalty, but cannot deny their love. Charles in Rome releases Christine with apparent readiness— is it not a priest he wants to be in any case? And there comes the meeting of Tommy and Krimmie in his garret, when they both sit silent, unwilling to utter words that will give pain, only to find that there is on each side a like confession to make.

They sat down together and after the longest, heaviest, most grievous silence he had ever known, he managed to start telling her. Suddenly he found her in tears, her face radiant, and heard her say: "You too?" He couldn't believe what he heard. "Do you mean?" he stammered. She nodded, blushed, and hid her head on his shoulder.

She gives him a startling view of feminine magnanimity when she invites him and Christine to luncheon together and presents her successor with a wedding ring. "The next day, Krimmie received a note from Tommy. He managed to answer it somehow. But he never heard from her again. Not even when she married the man 'out west.' If she ever married him at all. . . . .''

After all, was Tommy simply lying to Krimmie, and there was no such man "out west," but she had guessed at the state of his heart, and given him the most charitable of relief? It is not a question which Mr. Kreymborg asks. And if it is there at all, it is between the lines. For he is an author who makes you read between the lines.

The lovers marry impulsively on seventeen dollars. And it is not so very long before the ghost of Charles comes between them. Krimmie becomes aware that his wife has made the wrong choice, and he will not hold her bound. And here again the suffering of man and wife, the division of their loves, only brought them closer together in sympathy and affection.

There were occasions when Krimmie could not hide the strain under which he labored in behalf of his share of their understanding, and Christine wished to stay with him and send Charles away. Between two men who needed her more than any human entity, her joyousness was being torn apart. It was a situation, presumably, for a woman much older in suffering and wisdom, but, as far as he was concerned, Krimmie was glad Christine was the one who had to face it. He must take his own weakness in hand and conduct it with every outward sign of serenity. By every law in nature, Charles and Christine had always belonged to each other. Krimmie had been the unconscious medium for bringing them together again, and it was now his province to remove himself and to see that Christine let him do so. This she refused to accept. As if giving and receiving had any concern in the matter. She had determined to wait until she could be sure there was someone else—to take care of Krimmie. He endeavored to laugh at such a whim, but she looked at him clearly and said: "Someone will come and be more to you than a dozen Christines." Krimmie tried to make believe that this could be true. . . . .

And oh—fairy tale!—it "could" be true, and it turned out so. For then came Dorothy!

It is not in general to be recommended that men publish their affairs of the heart. But if they must do so—and it is clear that in our day they often must—let it be in this manner. This is the manner of one trained in the niceties of poetry—conception and wording. What this most resembles in American literature is some of the dramatic idyls of Mr. Frost, The Death of the Hired Man and The Generations of Men. If we have in *Troubadour* a notable augury for American prose, it is a reminder of how for the present age the pace has been set by the poets.

"A STORY-TELLER'S STORY"

Another book of autobiography that heartens the seeker after prose-writing of distinction is again the work of a poet, Mr. Anderson's *A Story-Teller's Story*. A less distinguished prose, it may be, as Mr. Anderson's *Mid-American Chants* are probably less distinguished verse. Or perhaps we should rather use the word "fastidious." His poems are certainly distinguished far beyond the ordinary. They are full of power; there is no failure to find images for thought or passion; there is no want of skill in weaving images into patterns. I am not certain that I do not take as much pleasure in the poems of Sherwood Anderson as in those of Rabindranath Tagore, to which they bear so much resemblance in mystical feeling and oriental imagery. But Tagore is a more cultivated poet, more sure of his effects, more fastidious.

It is not that Mr. Anderson does not take pains, and that he does not take pains with what is at the very heart of fastidious writing, with "the little tricky words." To doubt that would be to doubt without reason what he so often says of his pursuit of words:

I am the tale-teller, the man who sits by the fire waiting for listeners, the man whose life must be led into the world of his fancies, I am the one destined to follow the little, crooked words of men's speech through the uncharted paths of the forests of fancy. What my father should have been I am to become. Through long years of the baffling uncertainty, that only such men as myself can ever know, I am to creep with trembling steps forward in a strange land, following the little words, striving to learn all the ways of the ever-changing words, the smooth-lying little words, the hard, jagged, cutting words, the round, melodious, healing words. All the words I am in the end to come to know a little and to attempt to use for my purpose have, at the same time, the power in them both to heal and to destroy. How often am I to be made sick by words, how often am I to be healed by words, before I can come at all near to man's estate!

Like Mr. Kreymborg, Mr. Anderson has given full credit to Gertrude Stein for her amusing and often significant experiments with English words, and that is a sign of one concerned for style, sensitive to new effects, and awake to the undeveloped potencies of words. In his Introduction to Miss Stein's *Geography and Plays*, he speaks of the sacrifice of popularity she has made "to go live among the little housekeeping words, the swaggering bullying street-corner words, the honest working, money-saving words and all the other forgotten and neglected citizens of the sacred and half-forgotten city." And he has certainly made an intimate acquaintance with many of these kinds of words, housekeeping and street-corner, cutting and smooth-lying, and round, melodious, and healing words, as intimate an acquaintance perhaps as Mr. Kreymborg himself. Only he did not have the background of Kreymborg, who, though he did live for twenty years in a cigar store and underneath an elevated railway, was none the less brought up on Mozart and Debussy, and was from the beginning the natural companion of

Pierrot and Columbine, of century-old bisque stat-
uettes, and who, while he never saw the country
until he was a grown man, knew by instinct how
"the willow nods." Mr. Anderson was brought up,
as he tells us, on cabbage soup. There was no
Aeolian Hall to train his taste, but only the alleys
and street-corners of some Winesburg, Ohio to
whisper secrets in his ear.

The point of likeness between the two artists is
that neither of them was ever contented with the
plausible facility of machine production in letters;
that each of them, at a tremendous sacrifice, has
kept seeking his own fashion of speech; that they
have both avoided scrupulously the ponderous and
obvious, the smart and flippant. And Mr. Anderson's own disabilities he has turned into shining
merits. Of all the writers we have been considering
in this volume, he is the one who gives the most un-
mistakable impression of representing America—
not, like so many writers, by lack of finish—but in
pervasive and characteristic tone and flavor.

Not, I say, by lack of finish. I do not say that
an academic reader may not find here and there in
Mr. Anderson, who has had little formal training,
occasional breaches of grammar and no little neglect
of certain of the prescriptions laid down for begin-
ners in rhetoric. But the breaches of grammar are

rare indeed, and the neglect of rhetorical prescriptions is such as to offend none but the teacher
of rhetoric. It does not leave the reader in doubt of
the meaning; it does not point to muddled thinking
or an affectation of fineness or wisdom. Mr. Anderson, to whom life comes through the five senses,
modified only by some mystical faculty which we
may provisionally call "imagination," has sedulous-
ly avoided the vocabulary of intellectual abstraction.
He deals very little in intellectual formulations of
experience. He does not pretend to explain life like a
scientist but to feel it like a sensitive man. He has,
for example, a sense of something coming about in
American life—in our social consciousness, in the
altered rating of human "values," in the whole
color and complexion of our minds as affected by the
new industrial conditions. He believes that we are
coming into a new phase of civilization as different
from that of the Augustan world as the Augustan
civilization was different from that of the Middle
Ages, or that from the civilization of Rome. But
what this difference is he cannot make clear in abstract terms, so as to make it understood by the
academic mind. We college men live still in the
Augustan—or at least in the Victorian—world. We
have had relatively little experience of the world in
which Mr. Anderson has grown up. We have not

had the training of the street-corner; we have not worked in factories; we have not written advertisements for Chicago syndicates; we have not consorted with carpenters, nor very much with painters, either of houses, of carriages, or of pictures. And unless we have, through some special grace, a predisposition to sense these weather signs of a new order as he senses them, we simply declare that he does not know history, that essential values remain constant from age to age, and that he has proved nothing.

It is certain that he has proved nothing, and perhaps his book (and his books) are the worse for even the ghost of a theory that vaguely haunts them. For the most part he avoids theory and the vocabulary of theory. He avoids the type of sentence in which, even in fiction, an intellectual cast is given to the account of circumstances, of character, and of the action itself. It is perhaps not that he avoids this type of sentence, but that his natural instinct, his mental process, lends itself to a syntax almost as simple as that of the Bible. There is in him none of that suave compactness that carries forward the narratives of Howells, smoothly and lightly, with all their freight of delicate psychology; none of that brisk competence of Mrs. Wharton, hard and bright as a diamond, flashing irony in the turn of a phrase. One has but to open at random any of our cleverer writers in the traditional manner to be reminded of the difference. Let it be a story of Miss Cather.

A beautiful soundness of body, a seemingly exhaustless vitality, and a certain "squareness" of character as well as of mind, gave Cressida Garnet earning powers that were exceptional even in her lavishly rewarded profession. Managers chose her over the heads of singers much more gifted, because she was so sane, so conscientious, and above all, because she was so sure. Her efficiency was like a beacon to lightly anchored men, and in the intervals between her marriages she had as many suitors as Penelope. Whatever else they saw in her at first, her competency so impressed and delighted them that they gradually lost sight of everything else. Her sterling character was the subject of her story.

Mr. Anderson never carries so neatly packed a freight of thought, of fact, of allusion; and his ideas are not so neatly dovetailed with rhetorical tools. His sentences are often just as long, or longer, and they are sometimes built up into more elaborate periods. But they are built up in a looser pattern, more like the pattern of lyric poetry, with the repetition of simple connecting phrases, and an easy gathering together at the end of items not so much of information as of sensation.

As I lay, deep buried in the hay in the barn on another fall day, and as the resentment—born in me through having been made the son of two decaying, gentle families—grew deeper and deeper, and also as the grateful warmth of the departed

[253]

summer—captured and held by the hay—stole over my body, cold from the day of tramping in the woods in a cold rain in pursuit of the squirrels—as the warmth took hold of my body, the scene of my actual birth hour, just depicted, faded. I fled from the field of fact and into the field of fancy.

Mr. Anderson is of course not alone in such a manner of writing. Allowing for differences in personal quality, dozens of contemporary writers, as well as some classics, might be cited as doing, each in his own way, something similar. D. H. Lawrence, Dorothy Richardson, John Dos Passos, are enough, without bringing in continental writers or the inevitable Joyce, to suggest a widespread disposition to present experience not in intellectual formulations (reinforced with dialogue), but in terms of images and sense impressions. There is bound, in such a shift of method, to be some loss and some gain. We are here concerned with the gain. There is certainly a gain in vividness, in color. The manner of Edith Wharton is engraving or pastel, so far as vividness is concerned; and by comparison we have in Mr. Lawrence and Mr. Anderson the warmth of oil and turpentine. And whatever the possibilities of Mrs. Wharton's method, there is something less dogmatic, less fictitious, less "notional" (as Newman would say), in Mr. Anderson's. He gives you much more the sense of *being there*, of being identified with the person and the scene.

AUGURIES

Mrs. Wharton is diabolically sure of herself. Mr. Anderson is forever setting himself forth as one groping, feeling his way, in the difficult arts of life and of letters.

I am the one destined to follow the little, crooked words of men's speech through the uncharted paths of the forests of fancy. What my father should have been I am to become. Through long years of the baffling uncertainty, that only such men as myself can ever know, I am to creep with trembling steps forward in a strange land. . . . . .

The devil! as Anderson would say, what have we here? Another Perceval, another Dümmling? One so little instructed in the features of the great world that when knights come riding through the forest he can take them for angels? One awkward and fumbling in the ways of the court; but who, through his very simplicity, is destined to behold the Holy Grail and all the symbolic mysteries of the House of the Fisherman? In our present search the Holy Grail is the spirit of America, and I know of no one in our time who has so caught in prose that pungent and elusive spirit. An American returning from the Old World—from the parks of England, the gardens of Italy, the granges and chateaux of France—however much he may love the cultivated beauty of Europe, he is overcome with emotion, as he rides across our continent, by the wildflowers growing rank beside the railroad tracks, even by the tamarack swamps, the fallen trees, and all the profusion and waste of a landscape fresh and unsubdued. This is the feeling one has in reading Sherwood Anderson. He renders the emotion of the prairies, of dark nights under the stars; we breathe in him the breath of great rivers and the very smell of river bottoms, broad, neglected, and stirring with life.

I do not mean to say that these are the subjects on which he spends his words. More often it is the streets of little towns, men sitting out in summer in front of the hotel, or swapping stories in the livery barn. But there is in the very movement of his prose something suggestive of the largeness and freedom of our country. There is in *A Story-Teller's Story* an open, flowing rhythm, as of one writing easily, without cramp and tension, such as it is hard to match in our prose, and still harder perhaps in our verse. It is this prose-writer, rather than the poets, who wears the wide, loose garment of Whitman. Sandburg is largely affected by Whitman, to be sure, in his spirit and his words. But Sandburg is in the movement of contemporary poetry, and he has a taste for ironic indirection, for brevity, sharpness of outline, and ingenious shapeliness of form. Sandburg is a maker of pictures, much of an imagist, dominated more than Whitman by the aesthetic interest of the studio. It is Anderson who follows Walt's injunction to "loaf and invite the soul." As Wordsworth's *Prelude* is described in the subtitle as "the growth of a poet's mind," *A Story-Teller's Story* is described as "the tale of an American writer's journey through his own imaginative world and through the world of facts." And the pleasure one derives from reading this prose autobiography is akin to the pleasure one derives from reading the rambling and leisurely *Prelude*. Only Wordsworth is a poet writing in his study and doing his best—a little anxiously—to give a philosophical formulation of his imaginative life which may be edifying to readers shut up in their studies. Whereas one recognizes in Mr. Anderson some type that one might encounter in a Pullman carriage, part actor, part business man, part mechanic, part Methodist minister: an easy, expansive, friendly, communicative man, who seems to give himself wholly to the occasion, in hearty democratic fashion, and yet somehow, in his occasional silences, his curious delicacies and vaguenesses of statement, seems to keep back a part of himself, to leave a curtain undrawn before some innermost chamber of the spirit. It is a three days' journey upon which you have embarked, and there is no hurry to get the story told. There will be many interruptions for luncheon and dinner, and the long oblivion of sleep. One need not say everything at once; there will be ample opportunity to return and pick up some dropped thread of narrative and explanation.

Mr. Anderson has the faculty of telling a story straight off, in stark and objective plainness, and some of his best stories—as in *Winesburg, Ohio*—are so delivered. But in general it is more characteristic of him to write stories that require a deal of explanation; he is touching the mysteries of men's souls—and so he must be forever putting in a word in the effort to make clear this or that in the attitude of a character, returning often to some earlier circumstance that will help us to an understanding. He is much aware of the counterpoint of life, of the contrasting interwoven strands of people and circumstance. The neatest and most poetic arrangement—like something in German music—is that in his tale entitled "Brothers": where he begins with himself in his house in late October with the leaves falling straight down heavily; he proceeds to the old man whom he met in the fog, who has the mania of identifying himself as a relative with every criminal or other notability who holds the columns of the Chicago papers; he then tells the story of the factory foreman in Chicago who killed his wife in the entryway; then back to the old man from the fog, who claims to be the brother of the murderer; and so again to himself in his house in the country with the leaves falling straight down heavily in the rain.

That is as simple as a folk-song or a minuet. More often Anderson develops a much more complicated idea, with many voices entering, some but once or twice, some as persistently as the several themes of a fugue. Sandburg proposes in one of his poems, "chants that repeat and weave." He is thinking perhaps of something in music, or more likely of Whitman's "Out of the Cradle Endlessly Rocking," or "When Lilacs Last in the Dooryard Bloomed." And the phrase suggests what Mr. Anderson does in *A Story-Teller's Story*, and especially in the first book. The general theme of this book is the likeness between the author and his father, the shiftless sign-painter in the little Ohio town, who was a born story-teller in a society not yet organized so as to have a place for the story-teller. In the first of the nine notes into which the book is divided, he gives a rapid sketch of the conditions of poverty in which the family lived, dwelling much upon the silent and beloved mother who kept the family going, and upon the games out of Cooper which the boys would play when the cabbages were gathered and securely stored away for winter provender. The father just makes his appearance here, painting up the fences of farmers with the name of Alf Granger the baker, and telling romantic and mendacious tales of his heroism in the Civil War. With the second note the story-telling father is taken up for serious development, and he is the central theme through the fifth, through a long series of fascinating pages which should take their place in American literature if nothing else of Anderson remains.

We hear first of his custom in the winter of going on the road with one companion to give some sort of vaudeville entertainment in country schoolhouses. But that is simply an introduction to the account of his story-telling about the stove of the farmhouse where he is being put up. Here it is not the author's intention to relate simply one of the stories told on such occasions by his father; his intention is, in this typical instance, to give an impression of the conditions, the emotional accompaniment, the impulse and process of story-telling in general, as well as to suggest the changing character of stories with changing times. And this he must do—such being his faculty and bent—not in the manner of the expository essayist, but with the concreteness of imaginative creation. His method is inevitably like what we call in dramaturgy "expressionism." Many things are going on at once, or as nearly at once as is compatible with the physical limitations of the printed page. There is the story itself which his father told, or would tell—a particular story presented in lieu of a type or a composite, a melodrama suitable to the moving pictures: the father for hero, the one member of an old aristocratic southern family who, because of his devotion to Abraham Lincoln, is separated from all he most loves; the escape from the southern house; the death of all his family at the hands of northern soldiers; and the battle of Gettysburg.

There is the feeling of his father as the story develops, the complete satisfaction of his aesthetic sense. There is the group of listeners: the farmer and his wife; the amazed comrade, Aldrich; and above all the enchanted hired girl, Tillie, who knows that the story-teller is chiefly addressing her, and who feels underneath it all the chivalrous attitude of the story-teller toward her as a virgin and his democratic sympathy for her as a hired girl. Perhaps I have not yet enumerated all the strands that go into this web. The author must set the stage; he must begin the story; he must remind the reader of how the father feels toward Tillie and how she feels toward him; he must get along with the story; he must return to the scene in the farmhouse

and the effect on the auditors in general; he must remind the reader that the story-teller is lying, and of
the satisfaction he takes in the artistic lie; he must
get along with the story; he must let the story-teller
indulge in sentimentalism over the purity of the
southern woman, or his destiny "to wander forever
stricken and forlorn through life," but determined
"to spend the remaining days of his life bringing
what sweetness and joy he could into the lacerated
hearts of a nation torn by civil strife." And at the
end the author must return to the entertainment in
the schoolhouse, a very poor entertainment offered
to a very scanty audience, and then the comforting thought of Tillie's appreciation of the story-
telling.

Even though the farmer and the farmer's wife should have
proved hard-hearted one remembers the number of Tillies in
the farmhouses of Ohio. When everything else failed the Tillies would have taken care of the troubadours. Of that one may
be, I should say, very very sure.

In the following notes of the first book, Mr.
Anderson relates in the same manner the occasion
when he first became aware, as a boy, of his own
bent for fictitious invention. The impulse was with
him a reaction against his father's type of melodrama, and was aroused by hearing his father give
an account of the circumstances of Sherwood's birth.

And Sherwood, plunged deep in the warmth of a haymow, tells himself a story of how he was born of a very different father under a very different sun. The wet day on a farm, the tramp through the woods, the haymow, his father's narrative, and his own invention are woven into a pattern of recurring strands almost as complicated as that of his father's story-telling by the farmhouse stove.

All this, as I set it down in its nakedness, sounds very complicated, very artificial and arranged, very intellectual and high-brow. And this is true enough in the sense that the author views his subject in several planes crossing at queer angles, inasmuch as he is presenting not merely a story but the process of story-telling. But in another sense, this is a more natural way of conducting narrative than the rigidly simplified and schematized procedure of the story-teller of literary tradition. The story-teller of literary tradition, in his simplification, has perhaps even more obviously arranged his material: with his neat and orderly progress, his careful explanation at the beginning of all that needs explaining so that he need not come in with intruding after-thoughts, his rigorous maintenance of chronological sequence. He is nearer the artificiality, or at any rate the intellectual rigor, of a logical syllogism. And Mr. Anderson has more often been accused of want of form

[263]

than of too much arrangement. He says at one point in the book:

However, I again find myself plunging forward into a more advanced and sophisticated point of view than could have been held by the boy. . . . . I shall be blamed. Those of my critics who declare I have no feeling for form will be filled with delight over the meandering formlessness of these notes.

In point of fact, whereas each of the two methods is a notable example of artistic control in the interest of form, this of Mr. Anderson's, in addition to being the one needed for presenting his theme, has, as you read, the beauty of seeming like the way stories are actually told by unprofessional masters of the craft. The easy beginning, without too much explanation, the frequent return to the farmhouse and the story-teller to remind the hearer of what the narrator is driving at, the return to a situation in the story already treated in order to add a stroke or two of vividness or significance, the sense of unhurried and unworried narrative—all this reminds one of the way people actually tell stories on Pullman trains or on long afternoons of idleness. It is in effect the manner of an old wives' tale. It has been beautifully simulated by some of our greatest story-tellers—by Defoe, for one, in *The Apparition of Mrs. Veal*. "I should have told you before," says the justice of peace in Maidstone, "that Mrs. Veal told Mrs. Bargrave that her sister and brother-in-law were just come down from London to see her." "All the time that I sat with Mrs. Bargrave, which was some hours, she recollected fresh sayings of Mrs. Veal. And one material thing more she told Mrs. Bargrave. . . . ." It was by such means that Defoe secured general credence for a ghost story which has no great element of interest except for its marvelous likeness in the telling to other ghost stories, and especially those given, with every attestation of authenticity, by the Society for Psychical Research.

Still more like is Mr. Anderson's method to that of Conrad where he employs the "Marlow device" —delegating to this shadowy man of the sea the business of inquiring further into the case of Lord Jim, of Mr. Kurtz, or of Flora de Barral, going still farther back as he gets new data from farther back, or capriciously leaping forward to a later point in the story, picking up dropped threads, and frequently reminding us of the circumstances under which Marlow was telling his story and of the feeling, sometimes of irritation and surliness, existing between him and his auditors. It is thus that Conrad leads us step by step into the heart of his mystery, or builds up touch by touch a portrait that is to be something so much more than a staring photograph. For Conrad and Anderson are alike in this:

that no circumstance in human nature is for them without its accompanying mystery, a thing to be caught in a net of words, but ever somewhat beyond words. They are like fishermen who keep their trout alive in the water even after it is caught in order that it may not lose the colors of a live fish. --.

Upon examination we find that such a method is eminently the product of skilful art. But as we listen to the telling we are rather impressed by the apparent artlessness. There is something so experimental and exploratory about this procedure, something ingenuous and convincing. The story-teller does not pretend to know everything. Such a story must be true, else the teller would not spend so much pains upon it, would not be so concerned to have you understand it in its minutest detail, in its last shade of implication. He is concerned, but not anxious; he takes his time. In his whole manner there is something reassuring, something calming to a nervous listener. There is a relish in the telling. You take a pleasure in the return to a situation already touched upon. Above all, in Anderson's story, you enjoy the return from his father's tale to the man himself telling his tale by the farmhouse stove, and the going back again from the teller to the tale.

The story-teller has got his audience leaning forward in their chairs. Outside the farmhouse in which they sit a wind begins to blow and a broken branch from a nearby tree is blown against the side of the house. The farmer, a heavy, stolid-looking man, starts a little and his wife shivers as with cold and Tillie is absorbed—she does not want to miss a word of the tale.

And now father is describing the darkness of the valley below the hill and the lights seen, far off. Will any of the little company of prisoners ever see their own homes again, their wives, their children, their sweethearts? The lights of the farmhouses in the valley are like stars in the sky of a world turned upside down.

The Rebel commander of the guard has issued a warning and a command: "It's pretty dark here, and if any of the Yanks make a stir to move out of the centre of the road fire straight into the mass of them. Kill them like dogs."

A feeling creeps over father. He is, you see, a southern man himself, a man of the Georgia hills and plains. There is no law that shall prevent his having been born in Georgia, although tomorrow night it may be North Carolina or Kentucky. But tonight his birthplace shall be Georgia. He is a man who lives by his fancy and tonight it shall suit his fancy and the drift of his tale to be a Georgian.

And so he, a prisoner of the Rebels, is being marched over the low hill, with the lights from distant farmhouses shining like stars in the darkness below, and suddenly a feeling comes over him, a feeling such as one sometimes has when one is alone in one's own house at night. . . . .

The farmer is nodding his head and his wife has her hands gripped, lying in her lap. Even Aldrich is awake now. The devil! Father has given this particular tale a new turn since he told it last. "This is something like." Aldrich leans forward to listen.

And there is the woman Tillie in the half-darkness. See,

she is quite lovely now, quite as she was on that evening when she rode with the horse dealer in the buggy! Something has happened to soften the long, harsh lines of her face and she might be a princess sitting there now in the half-light.

Father would have thought of that. It would be something worth while now to be a tale-teller to a princess. . . . .

And now the weary prisoners with their escort have come down off the hillside to a valley, and are approaching a large old southern mansion, standing back from the road they have been traveling, and the officers in charge of the prisoners—there were two of them—command the guards to turn in at a gate that leads to the house. . . . .

So there was father, sitting comfortably in the warm farmhouse living room—he and Aldrich having been well fed at the table of a prosperous farmer—and having before him what he most loved, an attentive and absorbed audience. By this time the farmer's wife would be deeply moved by the fate of that son of the South that father had represented himself as being; and as for Tillie—while, in the fanciful picture he is making, he stands in the cold and wet outside the door of that southern mansion, Heaven knows what is going on in poor Tillie's heart. It is, however, bleeding with sympathy, one may be sure of that.

So there is father and, in the meantime, what of his own actual flesh-and-blood family, the family he had left behind in an Ohio village when he set forth on his career as an actor?

It is not suffering too much. One need not waste too much sympathy on his family. . . . .

The transitional phrases, the phrases of return and recapitulation, are naturally not of the stiff and formal kind called for by expository writing. There is nothing of the forensic manner of a Macaulay proceeding from one topic to another. It is all easy and simple:

And now he is in the farmhouse. . . . . And then father would have described: . . . . And now the weary prisoners with their escort. . . . . But, as you will understand quickly enough. . . . . So there was father, sitting comfortably in the warm farmhouse. . . . . And so, you see, father went back again to his old home after all. . . . . There was the night and the rain, and father, with a dark cloak about his shoulders. . . . . You will understand that the young man now dying lived in that very house, far back from the road, toward which father went that night when he escaped the Rebel guard. He had marched off with the stick over his shoulder, you will remember, and had then cut off across fields to his own home where he was concealed by the negroes until the night of his final escape.

There is Marlow's desire that you shall understand both the physical and the psychological posture of affairs, and not merely that you shall understand them with your mind but that you shall appreciate them, shall see them, shall feel them. Each time the situation is rephrased, not merely to keep you *au courant*, but to remind you of the picture: "There was the night and the rain, and father now with a dark cloak about his shoulders, creeping from the stables and toward the house."

It is too often the way of story-tellers to consider words as counters of thought; the word tells you what you need to know and there's an end of it.

The reason Mr. Anderson admires Gertrude Stein is that she does not take words as mere counters of thought, that she realizes so well how much they mean as entities in the physical world, sending waves of energy as it seems straight to our imagination without the interposition of our reason. That is, if they are the right words and rightly set in order. Unfortunately, Miss Stein has carried her experiments so far that few people take her seriously, however many may have been amused by her cleverness or actually influenced by her technique. She has been too freakish, too well content to let her words go their way and weave their own fantastic patterns, without regard to any central imaginative control. But Mr. Anderson admires her, and he may have learned from her certain important little lessons.

He has learned, for example, not to be afraid to repeat a word or phrase when there is occasion for it. The old-line writer thinks that a word is an idea, and that the idea once communicated, he may leave it to the reader to keep it in mind. Mr. Anderson realizes that a word may be a stimulus to the imagination, and that there are often cases where the stimulus should be repeated as a phrase in music is repeated, or as one goes on tapping on a nail until he has driven it in. He has learned that there are words and phrases entirely unnecessary to convey his idea to the reader, and yet most helpful in communicating his feeling, in appealing to that complex of nervous reactions in which the psychologist locates the soul. Suppose he wants to tell us of the three Anderson boys, of how they go to bed on a winter night, undressing in the kitchen, fighting for the warmest place in their common bed, and having their chapped hands greased by their mother. I have put it all in a sentence because I am in a hurry and because the reader may find it all set forth in *A Story-Teller's Story;* and I have failed to give any of these words their due imaginative effect. But the author himself cannot afford to present the facts in any such schematic outline. The reader would have the facts, but they would mean practically nothing at all to him. Let the reader turn to the book; I cannot afford to quote more than a bit or two of this beautiful piece. Here is, however, one bit:

> The three boys are in the bed in the room and there are not enough bedclothes. Father's overcoat, now too old to be worn, is thrown over the foot of the bed and the three boys have been permitted to undress downstairs, in the kitchen of the house, by the kitchen stove.

There are here many words and phrases unnecessary for communicating the idea. For that purpose it might just as well have read, and many readers will no doubt so prefer it:

The three boys are in bed and there are not enough bedclothes. Father's overcoat, now too old to be worn, is thrown over the foot of the bed and the boys have been permitted to undress downstairs by the kitchen stove.

There is surely no need to tell us that a bed is in a room, or that the kitchen stove is in "the kitchen of the house." There is no need to say "in the bed" where the idea is simply that they were "in bed." And there is no need to tell us a second time—it is really, in the book, the fourth or fifth time—that there are three boys. But the author is not primarily concerned with letting us know the facts of the case. As for the facts, they are sufficiently set forth in passages preceding and following this paragraph. All the facts set forth in this chapter could have been adequately covered, for purposes of information, in three pages instead of the twenty actually employed. The author is primarily concerned with the atmosphere of those times, that strange, elusive thing which we call the "feel" of life. To take the most crucial instance, the phrase, "in the bed," which occurs several times like that in the three or four pages involved—suppose he had said "in bed." "In bed" is an abstraction with a definite meaning sufficient for the case so far as the facts are concerned. But "in the bed" is an image, rendering something much more concrete to the imagination. They were not merely in bed, they were in that bed, and that bed, as the author wants us to remember, is "in the room." He does not have to describe the room, as so many writers would have done, in all its chilly bareness and meanness. He has told us enough about that family to give us a notion of the sort of room it would be. But he does want us to have the sense of that bed as being in that room.

And the same with "the kitchen of the house," a phrase so unnecessary to the thought. There are three successive steps in our introduction to the locale of the boys' undressing, each adding its mite of suggestion to the picture, to the emotion which accompanies such a picture. They were permitted to undress "downstairs, in the kitchen of the house, by the kitchen stove." It is perhaps sufficient for my purpose to call attention to the rhythm of the thing, the cadence of that wavelike, threefold phrase, which would be spoiled by omitting the words, "of the house." But there is more to it than that. It is of course possible that Mr. Anderson is here simply employing the colloquial, and especially the southern colloquial, redundancy that makes "the kitchen of the house" a natural mouth-filling equivalent of kitchen. And that would be amply justified in this place. But I fancy there is here, as in the words, "in the room,'" the intention of insisting on "the house" as a part of the sensational and emotional complex. The Andersons, owing to their poverty, seldom occupied the same house for many months at a time, and the houses they occupied were haunted houses, which less needy people would not take. This we already know, and I believe that something of this is to be felt in the phrase which carries with it more than the simple idea—or the simple image——kitchen. The significant thing is that this prose-writer dares to use these words so unnecessary for the communicating of the idea and to repeat them more than once, in the same spirit in which a poet uses and repeats unnecessary words, following what is the basic principle of musical composition. Sometimes they are repeated without modification, and sometimes, as with Milton's repetition of the name "Lycidas" in the first stanza of his elegy, with variation and an increment of words working up emotional effect. A little later in this chapter Mr. Anderson is speaking of the mother warming a dish of fat with which to rub the chapped hands of the three boys, and he says: "For an hour she has had the dish sitting at the back of the kitchen stove in the little frame house far out at the edge of the town." And there we have reached the limit of the development of that theme of the house.

As for the second reference to the three boys, that is another of the themes the author is developing in his tender, reminiscent evocation of childhood days. He is not concerned with the idea "boys" so much as the image "three boys"—an image charged with emotion, for one thing, because one of them, the youngest, who so much resembled their silent mother, had since "mysteriously disappeared out of our lives and never come back." Each reference to the three boys is like a caress; it is the caress of a lover, or the loving stroke of an artist. And when the author says of the boys in bed, "The youngest brother of the three brothers has already taken one of the two outside positions. It is his fate," I cannot think that it is an affectation to say "the youngest brother of the three brothers" instead of "the youngest of the three brothers," or simply "the youngest brother." I must think it is a stroke of art, one of those loving and individual touches by which we distinguish the work of a human craftsman from the work of a machine.

Here, then, is a writer of imaginative prose who dares to use some of the common devices of the poet, of the composer of music, of the painter of pictures. He dares to repeat at this and that point in his picture the note of color that he wants distributed so. He dares even to put down a sentence without a verb, as the painter prides himself on giving us a figure without completing the sharp outline from head to heel. He dares to arrange the elements not according to the rigid economy of exposition but according to the rich freedom of sentiment and imagination. At rare moments, when the subject calls for it, he approaches the very movement of poetry, not the meter, but what we may call the "rhetorical rhythm" of poetry. In this first chapter of *A Story-Teller's Story*, the boys are fighting for the best position in the bed.

But there is now the sound of the mother's footsteps on the stairs and that is the end of the struggle. Now—at this moment—the boy who has the coveted position may keep it. That is an understood thing.

The mother puts the kerosene lamp on a little table by the bed and beside it a dish of warm, comforting melted fat. One by one six hands are thrust out to her.

There is a caress in her long toil-hardened fingers.

In the night and in the dim light of the lamp her dark eyes are like luminous pools.

The fat in the little cracked china dish is warm and soothing to burning itching hands. For an hour she has had the dish sitting at the back of the kitchen stove in the little frame house far out at the edge of the town.

The strange, silent mother! She is making love to her sons, but there are no words for her love. There are no kisses, no caresses.

The rubbing of the warm fat into the cracked hands of her sons is a caress. The light that now shines in her eyes is a caress.

. . . .

The silent woman has left deep traces of herself in one of her sons. He is the one now lying stilly in the bed with his two noisy brothers. What has happened in the life of the mother? In herself, in her own physical life, even the two quarreling, fighting sons feel that nothing can matter too much. If her husband, the father of the boys, is a no-account and cannot bring money home—the money that would feed and clothe her children in comfort—one feels it does not matter too much. If she herself, the proud quiet one, must humiliate herself, washing—for the sake of the few dimes it may bring in—the soiled clothes of her neighbors, one knows it does not matter too much.

And yet there is no Christian forbearance in her. She speaks sometimes as she sits on the edge of the bed in the lamplight rubbing the warm fat into the cracked frost-bitten hands of her children and there is often a kind of smoldering fire in her words.

Of course Mr. Anderson is not our sole example of such liberal treatment of prose. There are, to mention no others, Mr. Waldo Frank and Mr. Ernest Hemingway, whose recent volume of sketches, *In Our Time*, has a certain neat, bright charm which is not to be ignored. Mr. Waldo Frank is particularly remarkable for his plunges into the undersurface life of the soul and for many novelties of technique, as in *City Block*, in rendering the feel of life in these unfrequented depths. But that is another story, and a long one. As for Mr. Hemingway, he stays too obstinately on the surface to touch us deeply even in what he might call our "aesthetic" sense. I take a considerable amount of pleasure in his description of Nick's fishing trip, and I recognize the art displayed in his account of his feelings after making camp:

> Inside the tent the light came through the brown canvas. It smelled pleasantly of canvas. Already there was something mysterious and homelike. Nick was happy as he crawled inside the tent. He had not been unhappy all day. This was different though. Now things were done. There had been this to do. Now it was done. It had been a hard trip. He was very tired. That was done. He had made his camp. He was settled. Nothing could touch him. It was a good place to camp. He was there, in the good place. He was in his home where he had made it. Now he was hungry.

This is clean, cool, competent writing. The man knows what he is about. But Mr. Hemingway, with his clever objectivity, with his not very serious irony, has not in this volume given evidence of more than a certain proficiency in technique. Mr. Anderson is a genius or nothing. He has not had the literary training of these other men. But he has a genial and opulent nature; and he is in touch with common human experience both above and below the surface.

[278]

AUGURIES

I could find faults enough with Mr. Anderson if I were so minded. I do not pretend to say that he has written prose as fine as Hazlitt or Ruskin. It is, as I have said, loosely woven. If prose is to be judged as tableware is judged, by its hardness, transparency, and glaze, or as rugs are valued, by the number of knots to the square inch, I am afraid we must declare at once that his work will not bring a high price in the market nor find an honored place in the cabinets of connoisseurs. But I am one who can take pleasure in Navajo blankets as well as in rugs of Khiva, and in Cantagalli china more even than in Sèvres and Dresden, since it is so often more attractive in design, and speaks so eloquently of the Tuscan soil, the mother-earth from which it is molded. And anyone on the lookout for American prose, home-made and savory, anyone eager for signs of promise for American prose, cannot afford to find fault with Sherwood Anderson until at least he has dwelt long upon his merits. If there is no hope in this direction, then where are we to look? I am strongly inclined to think that we have more than hope here, that we have gratifying accomplishment. And this is the more interesting because, as in the case of Kreymborg, the impulse to this prose is so like the impulse to contemporary poetry in America. If the nearest affinity to Kreymborg's

THE OUTLOOK FOR AMERICAN PROSE

prose is the poetry of Frost, the nearest affinity to Anderson's prose is the poetry of Sandburg. And if the poets have taken the lead in this new movement in American literature, here are signs that the writers of prose will not be long in following them.

DECEMBER, 1925

[280]

INDEX OF AUTHORS

INDEX OF AUTHORS

INDEX OF AUTHORS

PRINTED IN THE U.S.A.